Inequa   th

What if B

Richard Mitchel

The POLICY PRESS

First published in Great Britain in September 2000 by

The Policy Press
34 Tyndall's Park Road
Bristol BS8 1PY
UK

Tel no +44 (0)117 954 6800
Fax no +44 (0)117 973 7308
E-mail tpp@bristol.ac.uk
www.policypress.org.uk

© The Policy Press and the Joseph Rowntree Foundation 2000

Published for the Joseph Rowntree Foundation by The Policy Press

ISBN 1 86134 234 9

Richard Mitchell is Senior Research Fellow and **Daniel Dorling** is Professor of Quantitative Human Geography, both at the School of Geography, University of Leeds, **Mary Shaw** is Research Fellow at the School of Geographical Sciences, University of Bristol.

The **Joseph Rowntree Foundation** has supported this project as part of its programme of research and innovative development projects, which it hopes will be of value to policy makers, practitioners and service users. The facts presented and views expressed in this report are, however, those of the authors and not necessarily those of the Foundation.

The statements and opinions contained within this publication are solely those of the authors and contributors and not of The University of Bristol or The Policy Press. The University of Bristol and The Policy Press disclaim responsibility for any injury to persons or property resulting from any material published in this publication.

The Policy Press works to counter discrimination on grounds of gender, race, disability, age and sexuality.

Cover design by Qube Design Associates, Bristol
Front cover: Photographs kindly supplied by Karen Bowler from The Policy Press and www.johnbirdsall.co.uk
Printed by the Alden Group, Oxford

Contents

Acknowledgements

The authors would like to thank the Joseph
Rowntree Foundation for supporting this research,
and in particular the research manager for the
project, Dominic Hurley. We are grateful to the
advisory committee for their invaluable advice:
Ian Baker, David Blane, Sarah Curtis, Seeromanie
Harding, Heather Joshi, Graham Moon and
Richard Wilkinson. We would like to thank the
publishing team and The Policy Press, in
particular Karen Bowler and Dave Worth.
Invaluable research assistance came from
Katherine French, Bethan Thomas and Nichola
Tooke. We would also like to thank Sally
Macintyre for access to the Medical Research
Council's Social and Public Health Sciences Unit.
Mary Shaw is funded by ESRC Fellowship Number
R000271045.

The Office for National Statistics and General
Register Office (Scotland) mortality data and the
Census data used in this report are Crown
Copyright.

List of tables and figures

Introduction

Aims

It has long been known that the circumstances in which people live and the manner in which society is organised affect how and when people die. The patterns of inequality in life expectancy between different places are not a matter of chance or fate, but a reflection of the stuff of life itself. This inequality is often referred to as 'the gap' – between rich and poor and, in Britain, between 'North' and 'South'. This report looks at *change* in those patterns of inequality – change which has occurred in recent times and change which might be brought about if current government policies succeed in making life in Britain more equal. The future is considered first, with analysis of the past and then methodological explanations following. The report's underlying theme is identification of the factors which account for patterns of inequality, and how these might be used as levers with which to narrow that 'gap'.

To begin, the report estimates the effect on death rates if life in Britain were changed through successful government policy initiatives. Each policy examined is a real and current one. This is not a 'blue sky' report; it is based on changes to life in Britain which may be happening *now*. Specifically, the report estimates the effects on inequalities in health of achieving full employment, of eradicating child poverty and of some modest redistribution of income. The effects of these changes are considered for the nation as a whole and on the constituency-level pattern of mortality. The report shows how big the reward for the effective implementation of progressive social policy might be. This, after all, is a government which wants to tackle 'the worst inequality of all': inequality in health (Dobson, 1997). These results can be found in Chapter 2.

The rest of the report takes a step-by-step approach to explaining contemporary inequalities in mortality, explaining how those inequalities have developed over time, and showing how policies of the past are implicated in those changes. The report explores the importance of social change on the pattern of premature mortality. It determines the extent to which changes that took place in society during the 1980s and early 1990s are responsible for the widening of inequalities in health seen now, and for changes in the geographical pattern of good and poor health. In particular, the report asks: in which places, and on which (social and demographic) groups did social change have most effect? Which factors best account for the changes in the geography of mortality over the period?

Background

The geography of mortality in Britain is well known, with higher death rates in the North and Scotland and in the inner areas of larger cities. Associations between the chances of an individual dying and their age, gender, social class and employment status are also quite clear. However, the way in which these demographic, socioeconomic and geographic factors interact to create the geography of mortality is less clearly understood.

Understanding the impact of social factors on health is important in an environment where political emphasis has been placed on reducing inequality, unemployment and child poverty. Levels of inequality and unemployment are largely the result of long-term government policy, albeit set against the background of a shifting global economy. This report shows how the cost of policy success or failure can be estimated in terms of the real number of lives potentially lost or saved. It builds on a very large body of established research to achieve this.

The first map (Figure 1) shows the changing pattern of the chances of premature death in Britain between the early 1980s and the early 1990s. Premature deaths (those which occur at ages less than 65) are used throughout the report as an indicator of poor health. At first glance the map looks rather strange – this is because it is a *cartogram*. Figure 2 shows what a cartogram is, and why the report uses them.

Figure 1 shows the pattern of change which the report tries to account for and which, it suggests, successful policy might alter. Likelihood of premature death is measured relative to the national average and is standardised to take into account differing age and gender profiles in each area. In the extreme eight constituencies – coloured red on the map – people's relative chances of dying before the age of 65 rose between 26% and 47% over the 10-year period of study. 'Relative' here means compared to the national average. Most of these very rapid rises occurred in areas such as Glasgow, Manchester and London, where mortality rates were already very high to begin with. At the opposite extreme, relative premature mortality rates fell by between 15% and 28% in five constituencies (coloured indigo).

It is important to be clear about the standpoint from which the report is written. The theory behind this research is that the map in Figure 1 shows mainly the legacy of social policies and social change in the late 1970s and 1980s. It is now almost universally accepted that this period was one of rapid social polarisation. The rich became very much richer and the poor became poorer. Unemployment reached levels not experienced since the 1930s and was highly concentrated in the North and in inner cities. Some of the highest ever rates of long-term unemployment were established in these areas. Child poverty rates and inequalities among children also rose rapidly. The policies and processes of change were geographically uneven in terms of who gained and who lost. Eventually this uneven impact became marked on almost all aspects of the human geography of the country, illuminated in this report via maps of premature mortality. At the extreme, the price of the social change in this period was that some people died

younger than they might have done under more equitable circumstances.

The extent to which that theory can be supported depends on how well measurable social changes account for the changing patterns of mortality shown in Figure 1. Much of this report explains how the theory was actually tested, how these ideas were operationalised and what was discovered. The final result of this process is the map in Figure 3 which shows what proportion of the changes seen in Figure 1 can be accounted for using the methods described here and in the technical report (available free from www.social-medicine.com).

To summarise, changes in mortality could be accounted for (to within 5%) in 95% of Britain's constituencies. Where Figure 3 is shaded light yellow to light blue either all the change is accounted for or there is very little change in mortality to account for and very little social change. Although, as the map shows, the change in some constituencies remains largely unaccounted for (notably inner cities in the North of Britain), the majority of mortality change *can* be accounted for by social change. This is a significant finding because it suggests that social conditions, changed through effective social policy, are levers by which the nation's health can be manipulated. If that is the case, and if social policy is altered in the right way, Britain's health could improve and a narrowing of the health gap could be possible.

Figure 1: Changes in death rates compared with the national average, parliamentary constituencies (early 1980s–early 1990s)

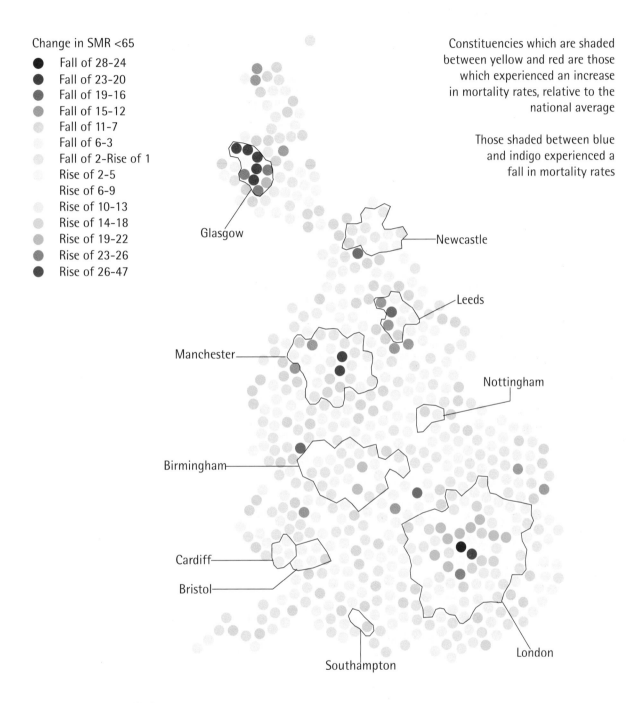

Change in SMR <65

- ● Fall of 28-24
- ● Fall of 23-20
- ● Fall of 19-16
- ● Fall of 15-12
- ○ Fall of 11-7
- ○ Fall of 6-3
- ○ Fall of 2-Rise of 1
- Rise of 2-5
- Rise of 6-9
- ○ Rise of 10-13
- ○ Rise of 14-18
- ○ Rise of 19-22
- ● Rise of 23-26
- ● Rise of 26-47

Constituencies which are shaded between yellow and red are those which experienced an increase in mortality rates, relative to the national average

Those shaded between blue and indigo experienced a fall in mortality rates

Glasgow

Newcastle

Leeds

Manchester

Nottingham

Birmingham

Cardiff

Bristol

Southampton

London

England and Wales SMR = 100

Figure 2: What is a cartogram and why have they been used?

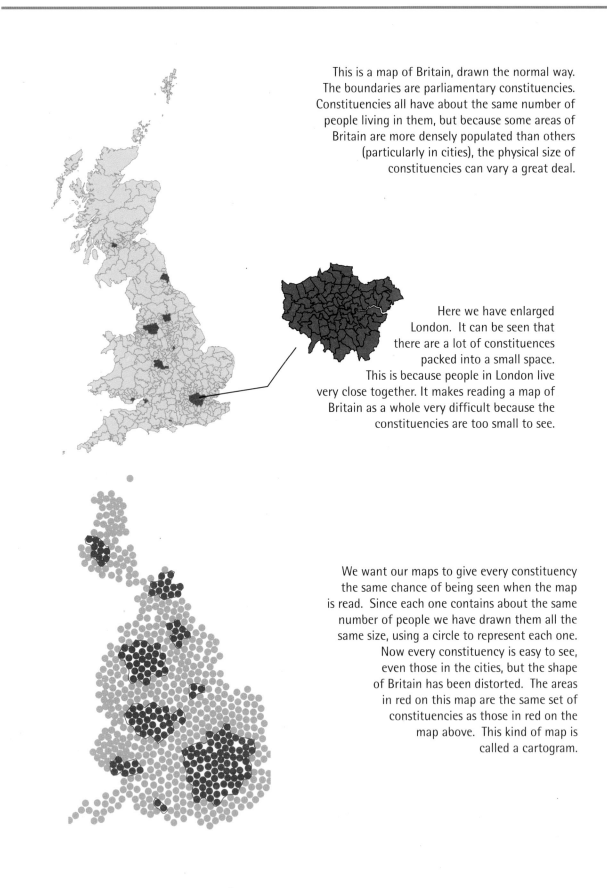

This is a map of Britain, drawn the normal way. The boundaries are parliamentary constituencies. Constituencies all have about the same number of people living in them, but because some areas of Britain are more densely populated than others (particularly in cities), the physical size of constituencies can vary a great deal.

Here we have enlarged London. It can be seen that there are a lot of constituences packed into a small space. This is because people in London live very close together. It makes reading a map of Britain as a whole very difficult because the constituencies are too small to see.

We want our maps to give every constituency the same chance of being seen when the map is read. Since each one contains about the same number of people we have drawn them all the same size, using a circle to represent each one. Now every constituency is easy to see, even those in the cities, but the shape of Britain has been distorted. The areas in red on this map are the same set of constituencies as those in red on the map above. This kind of map is called a cartogram.

Figure 3: Explaning the change in mortality (1983–93)

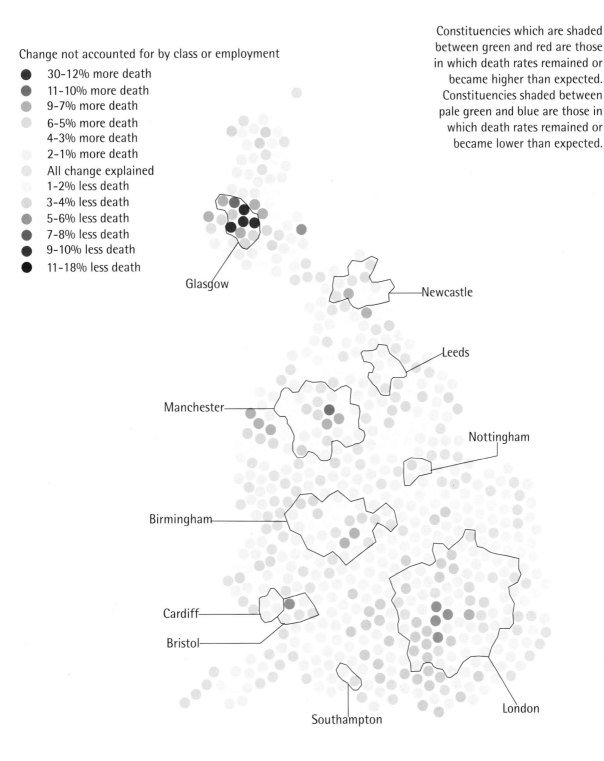

Change not accounted for by class or employment

- ● 30–12% more death
- ● 11–10% more death
- ● 9–7% more death
- ● 6–5% more death
-   4–3% more death
- ● 2–1% more death
- ● All change explained
-   1–2% less death
- ● 3–4% less death
- ● 5–6% less death
- ● 7–8% less death
- ● 9–10% less death
- ● 11–18% less death

Constituencies which are shaded between green and red are those in which death rates remained or became higher than expected. Constituencies shaded between pale green and blue are those in which death rates remained or became lower than expected.

Glasgow

Newcastle

Leeds

Manchester

Nottingham

Birmingham

Cardiff

Bristol

Southampton

London

Methods

To conduct the type of analysis presented in this report, two items of information were needed: first, the number of people who died in each area of Britain at each time point, together with their gender and age at death and, second, the number of people of each gender and age who were living in each area. If the size of a group of a given age and gender is known, as well as the number of that group who die in a given time period, the chances of death for any member of the group can be calculated – this is called their mortality rate. If the rates for different groups are pooled together in the correct way a *standardised mortality ratio* is produced (explained further in Chapter 4). A standardised mortality ratio (SMR) is a simple way of assessing the mortality rate in a particular constituency relative to the national average, taking into account the age and gender structure of that particular constituency. If the SMR is 100, the chances of death there are the same as the national average. If the SMR is higher than 100, the chances of death are higher and if it is lower than 100, the chances of death are lower. The further away from 100, the more extreme the deviation of the mortality rate from the average.

To explain why SMRs vary from area to area more information is needed about factors, other than the age and gender of an area's population, which might influence rates of death. An enormous amount of work has been undertaken on this, suggesting that one of the most important factors is the social class composition of an area – in simple terms, how many of the people living in the area are rich or poor. Poorer people die, on average, at higher rates than richer people so, if an area contains a high proportion of poorer people, the death rate in that area is likely to be high. A similar difference in the rates of death exists between employed and unemployed people. Since areas differ markedly in their class composition and in levels of unemployment, knowing about the class or employment status of an area's population can explain a lot about the rates of death there.

Behavioural factors, such as how much different groups of people smoke or drink or what they tend to eat, are not directly taken into consideration in this report. There are three reasons for this. First, these factors can be strongly associated with social class, age and gender. For example, the poorer you are the more likely you are to smoke and the more obstacles there are to giving up. Second, the geographical inequalities in behaviour are not, so far as is known, as strong as those of social class or employment status. The high number of (rich) City traders in London who smoke and eat poorly is a fine example of this. Third, there is relatively little reliable geographical information about behaviour available. We do not know the detailed geography of smoking rates by age and gender and social class across Britain in the 1970s and 1980s.

Some people may be surprised by the omission of behaviour from this analysis, but were these omissions to have mattered greatly then there would have been a much larger amount of unaccounted-for change shown in Figure 3. Since the models used in this report worked very well, without including behaviour, we believe that these omissions were warranted.

Report summary

What is in the rest of the report?

- Chapter 2 – presents the effects of three key policy objectives in terms of their impact on Britain as a whole, and on the geographical pattern of premature death.
- Chapter 3 – presents results to indicate how much of the changing pattern of inequalities in health can be accounted for by changes in the power of social class and employment to determine the geography of premature mortality.

Chapters 4, 5 and 6 take a step-by-step approach to explaining how our results have been obtained, the methods employed and the concepts behind those methods.

- Chapter 4 – explains the relationship between the chances of premature death and age, gender, social class and employment status in Britain, and how these produce the geographical inequalities seen in Britain today.
- Chapter 5 – explains how British society changed between the early 1980s and early 1990s, in terms of its structure, geography and the 'gap' between the most and least healthy parts of the country.
- Chapter 6 – explains how the results in this report were produced, discusses the data and calculations which lie behind them, and

assesses the reliability of the results.
- Chapter 7 – presents a brief review of the report.
- Appendix A – presents results for every constituency in Britain.
- Appendix B – discusses the evidence of the widening health gap.

Chapter summary

In this chapter the contents of the report have been outlined and some results have been presented.

- The report has two key aims: to determine how much of the *change* in patterns of premature mortality in Britain can be explained by social changes and to estimate the potential impact of three current government policies on health inequalities in Britain.
- Results for the first aim have been presented in the form of two maps (Figures 1 and 3). They show that the change in mortality rates can be accounted for (to within 5%) in 95% of Britain's constituencies through understanding social changes.
- The methods used in the report hinge on understanding the relationship between social class, employment status and the chances of dying, together with knowledge about how the distribution of different social classes and unemployment has changed over time.
- The report has not included behavioural factors (such as smoking and drinking) in accounting for these patterns, but this exclusion is justified and appears to have had no discernible impact on the results.

In the next chapter, the relationship between an individual's characteristics and their chance of dying is explored, together with how this helps to account for the *geography* of mortality in Britain.

2

Policy implications

In Chapter 1, maps showed that changes in the geography of mortality in Britain can largely be accounted for by social change (results which will be expanded upon in Chapter 3). This is a significant finding because it suggests that wider government policies which influence social change could have an effect on reducing Britain's unequal distribution of health, as expressed through premature death. Three broad aspects of social policy are examined in this chapter to illustrate what those effects could be.

Background

An historical view of Britain's health reveals that geographical inequalities were lower and fell during periods of more progressive and inclusive government policy. The largest and quickest fall in these inequalities occurred in the period between 1939 and 1950 (Dorling, 1995, Figure 5.31). When exactly the levels of inequality fell and what was responsible for that fall are disputed, but it is unquestionable that people's chances of dying were far more equitable by 1950 than they were just before the outbreak of the Second World War. The chances of premature death *can* be rapidly equalised. This period of improvement coincided with some of the most radical and rapid improvements in social equalities experienced in Britain during the last century. Events between 1950 and 1980 also suggest that when social equity grew, geographical inequalities in health diminished. The clearest relationship is that between income inequality and spatial inequality in mortality. Both inequalities were lowest when measured for the period between 1969 and 1973 (Shaw et al, 1999, Figure 4.5). Social change in the 1960s led to society being more equal in terms of wealth and health at that time.

The period between the early 1980s and the early 1990s had a very different policy context to the previous 30 years. With hindsight it is not difficult to understand how the social and economic policies of that decade helped to build a less equal society and led to the widest geographical inequalities in health ever measured in Britain – and now the widest in Western Europe (Shaw et al, 2000). Policies introduced in the early 1980s have sometimes been described as a social and economic experiment. Although they were clearly a resounding success for some, none of the architects of policy at the time could have conceived that the result would also be the legacy of inequality in life and death documented here. "There is no such thing as society", claimed Margaret Thatcher, but the changes wrought on 'society' by social policy allowed the rich to get much richer and enjoy remarkable falls in their risk of premature death, while the poor fared less well. If society does not exist, how then was it influenced and changed so profoundly? The policies were designed under the impression that the wealth and health of the rich would trickle down to the poor, but this did not happen. Instead, mass unemployment was allowed to grow and become established while welfare benefits were reduced; inequalities between social classes widened rapidly. This had a particularly damaging effect on poorer children and their health.

Government policies of the 1980s and early 1990s had a direct impact on the factors which are used in this report to account for spatial inequalities in health. By allowing inequalities in wealth and income to rise, the meaning and importance of social class was changed. Belonging to class I in the 1990s meant that a person was, on average, very much richer than they would have been in the 1980s because the class as a whole became much richer. Belonging to class V in the 1980s meant being poor relative to other classes, but by the 1990s it was more likely to mean being on the breadline. These changes were reflected in growing differences in mortality rates between the classes.

The effect of policy on unemployment mirrors the geography of death. As explained in Chapter 4, research has shown that people who are unemployed are more likely to die prematurely than their employed peers, in the years which follow redundancy (all else being equal). Those who are unemployed for a long time are *much* more likely to die prematurely. So, when government allowed unemployment to rise to unprecedented levels at unprecedented rates, and with those rises concentrated in particular parts of the country, growing inequality in the risk of premature death across Britain came as no surprise. The effect of the rapid de-industrialisation of Britain in the early 1980s is not best measured by jobs lost, but by the lives which were cut short as a result of 'letting the market decide'.

What of government policy now? The current government has not been in power for long, particularly in terms of the timescale needed to measure changes to inequalities in health which might stem from social policy. However, they have made many public statements of intent and policy, the results of which will not be known for some time. In the meantime it would be useful to *predict* what the actual outcome of these policies might be and that is what the rest of this chapter does.

Below, three major long-term policy goals are evaluated in terms of how their achievement might influence the levels of inequalities in death seen across Britain. These estimates should be treated with caution, since prediction of any kind is notoriously difficult. In every case, the predictions made are conservative and the impacts of successful policy implementation might be much larger. The models assume that many other aspects of life remain the same and that the relative levels of influence of particular social conditions also remain stable, but the estimates do allow the importance of these three broad policy goals to be compared and valued in terms of avoiding premature mortality – saving lives under the age of 65.

The models have been constructed using the early 1990s population as a base. Where figures are given for 'lives saved', they are thus not referring to the future per se. Population projections are simply not sophisticated enough to facilitate calculations of lives saved in, for example, 2020. Nonetheless, they give a detailed picture of the possible impact of social policy on death rates across the country – all else being equal.

Full employment for all

What if the government's stated aim of achieving employment for all those who want a job was achieved? How many lives might be saved, where, and with what effect on the overall picture of inequalities in premature death across Britain?

To estimate the effect of achieving full employment on death in Britain, a model used to explain the geography of mortality (see Chapter 3) has been modified – everyone who was unemployed has been given a job. The approach is described in more detail in the technical report, but is essentially very simple: the mortality rates of the unemployed have been altered to match those experienced by the employed. The adjustment was carried out only for men and women between the ages of 16 and 64 since one cannot be unemployed before 16, and it is unusual following retirement (for convenience, and due to likely harmonisation in the future, women's age of retirement has been raised to mirror men's). Although definitions of full employment vary, the government's version hinges on 'employment opportunity for all'. It is reasonable to assume that some people may be temporarily unemployed under conditions of 'full employment', but they should be between jobs rather than in long-term unemployment.

The results of removing all unemployment from the model of mortality are shown in Table 1.

In total, 2,504 lives would be saved per year (among those aged between 16 and 64) if full employment were attained. The effect would be most marked among men, with 3% (2,090) of premature deaths being prevented. Overall, the policy would result in 2% fewer deaths at these ages, for men and women in Britain. The table also shows the concentrated effect of full employment on death in those parts of the country which currently experience death rates

How to read the table

- The first row of the table gives the number of lives saved per year, through the attainment of full employment. Figures are given separately for men, for women and then as a combined total. This gives an idea of the numbers of deaths involved.

- The second row expresses the figures from the first row as a percentage of all the deaths in Britain (at ages 16-64). This gives an idea of the numbers of lives saved, compared to the number of deaths which take place across Britain in one year.

- The third row gives the number of lives saved per year in just those constituencies which have higher numbers of deaths than the national average. These are Britain's unhealthiest areas and are where the most action is needed if geographical inequalities are to be tackled.

- The bottom row is slightly more complicated. Again, the number refers to all those constituencies in which the number of deaths is higher than the national average, but this time the figure is based on the number of deaths which occur over and above that national average. These are called 'avoidable deaths' because they are attributable to factors other than age and gender and represent the deaths which might be prevented if everyone enjoyed the same good standards of wealth and health. The figure itself expresses the number of lives saved by full employment as a proportion of these avoidable deaths.

Table 1: What if full employment were achieved?

Population aged 16–64	Men	Women	Total
Lives saved per year in Britain	2,090	414	2,504
% lives saved in Britain	3	1	2
Lives saved per year in areas of excess mortality	1,432	270	1,702
% avoidable deaths prevented in areas of excess mortality	21	8	17

Note: Figures are rounded.

higher than the national average. As a whole, 17% of the unexpected and needless deaths which occur in these areas would be prevented just by this policy, with that figure rising to 21% among men only. In plain terms, this means full employment would (albeit indirectly) prevent about one in five of the needless deaths which take place among 15-64 year old men in Britain's least healthy areas. This concentration of the beneficial effects of the policy, in the more and most needy areas, would help to reduce substantially the *geographical* inequalities in British mortality rates.

The number of lives saved if this policy goal were achieved is considerable. Imagine if instead of tolerating mass long-term unemployment the governments of the 1980s and 1990s had implemented policies to move towards full employment – a decade of thousands of premature deaths would have been prevented.

Understanding the way the impact of this policy can be measured is perhaps easier with a specific example. Here we give figures which show what the impact of achieving full employment on Tony Blair's constituency could be (Table 2).

How to read the table

- The first row gives the difference between the absolute number of deaths which actually occurred in Sedgefield and the number which ought to have occurred if Sedgefield had mortality rates equal to the national average – these are the avoidable deaths discussed prior to Table 1.

- The second row gives the number of avoidable deaths which would still occur if full employment were attained (premature deaths unaccounted for by age/gender/social class).

- The third row shows the number of lives to be saved per year, in Sedgefield, through the attainment of full employment (the difference between the first two rows).

- The last row shows the proportion of avoidable deaths which would be 'avoided' in Sedgefield by the attainment of full employment.

Table 2: The impact of full employment on Sedgefield (per year)

Population aged 15–64	Men	Women	Total
Actual number of deaths above the national average (avoidable deaths)	+18	+13	+31
Number of deaths above the national average if there were full employment	+14	+12	+26
Lives saved per year	4	1	5
% of avoidable deaths prevented by full employment	20	7	16

Note: Figures are rounded.

Table 2 shows that just over one in six of the avoidable deaths in Sedgefield could be prevented by attaining full employment there. In a full five-year term, the Prime Minister and his government might keep an extra 25 constituents alive. The table shows that effect is more marked for men than women, reflecting the higher rates of unemployment among men.

A modest redistribution of wealth

Tony Blair stated, "I believe in greater equality", when he took office. Suppose that the government managed to reduce levels of inequality to those experienced in the early 1980s, when they were lower (although still historically very high). This would be a modest goal and quite achievable. Actions such as the introduction of the national minimum wage have gone some way towards a more equitable distribution of income and Chancellor Gordon Brown declared that the budget of 21 March 2000 would redistribute wealth. What if such policies were

continued and the social and financial gap between the social classes was reduced to the levels experienced in the early 1980s? Can we measure the influence this would have on the health divide?

Again, a simple approach is adopted to model the achievement of this goal. An assumption is made that a redistribution of wealth could reduce inequality in mortality rates between the social classes to those levels experienced in the early 1980s. To operationalise this idea the mortality rates of people in social class I are left unchanged at their 1990s level but the differences in mortality rates between those enjoyed by class I and those in other classes are then fixed at the level they were in the early 1980s. This approach combines the overall rise in standards of living between the 1980s and 1990s, with a reduction in the differential impact of that rise on different classes. The national results of achieving this mild redistribution are shown in Table 3. (The table is very similar to Table 1 so please refer to the instructions for reading Table 1).

Table 3: What if there was a slight redistribution of wealth across Britain?

Population aged <65	Men	Women	Total
Lives saved per year in Britain	5,734	1,864	7,597
% lives saved in Britain	8	4	7
Lives saved per year in areas of excess mortality	2,982	955	3,938
% avoidable deaths prevented in areas of excess mortality	43	26	37

Note: Figures are rounded.

The effect of even a modest redistribution of wealth on inequalities in health is very large indeed. 7,500 people aged under 65 would not die *per year* were material inequalities to fall slightly. Within the areas of Britain which have mortality rates higher than the national average, 43% of the male avoidable deaths which occur there would be prevented. Inequalities in health between different areas of Britain would fall rapidly, all else being equal.

How can such a slight redistribution of wealth have such a large overall effect? A great deal of the underlying inequalities in death between different parts of Britain are actually the reflection of social inequalities between people belonging to different classes and thus experiencing different life chances. *Everyone* is affected by their social class. If the effects of class are changed just a little this has a very large effect overall because that change affects *everyone*. Redistribution of wealth and opportunity has a bigger effect than providing full employment because unemployment only directly affects a minority of the population.

As before, a focus on Sedgefield helps to put more meaning on these figures.

Table 4 shows that about 65 constituents would

be saved from dying prematurely by this policy, in a five-year term of office. The table also shows that Sedgefield's high mortality rates would be brought a long way back towards the national average through the effects of this policy. This is another good example of the report's argument that this policy will help to reduce *geographical* inequalities in mortality because the proposed policies will have most impact in areas with higher death rates.

An end to childhood poverty?

The third aim of the government tested here is the eradication of child poverty. This is one of their flagship policies and almost no one would dispute its importance. What if it were achieved? Currently, the government believes that just under one third of children grow up in poverty in Britain. Again, the report uses the most straightforward method of simulating the effects of delivering on this policy.

A simple way to estimate the effect of ending childhood poverty is to give children in social classes IV and V the same good chances of health which those children in 'higher' classes currently enjoy. To do this, the poorest 20% of children were reassigned to higher social classes on a pro-

Table 4: The impact of mild redistribution of wealth on Sedgefield (per year)

Population aged <65	Men	Women	Total
Actual number of deaths above the national average (avoidable deaths)	+18	+13	+31
Number of deaths above the national average if there were redistribution	+9	+9	+18
Lives saved per year	9	4	13
% excess mortality avoided	53	29	43

Table 5: What if child poverty was eradicated across Britain?

Population aged 0-14	Boys	Girls	Total
Lives saved per year in Britain	1,183	224	1,407
% lives saved in Britain	30	8	21
Lives saved per year in areas of excess mortality	614	114	727
% avoidable deaths prevented in areas of excess mortality	100	33	92

Note: Figures are rounded.

rata basis and thus given a lower risk of death. In this instance, pro-rata means that if 15% of children in a constituency were in class II, and 100 children were in classes IV and V, 15 of them were 'elevated' to enjoy the risk of mortality associated with being in class II. (Note: this report actually uses a smaller group of children in poverty than the government's own estimates.) Although this is a somewhat crude procedure it does realistically reproduce the aims of eradicating childhood poverty: to bring the life chances of the poorest in line with those of the better off. The effects of achieving this policy are shown in Table 5.

Even though death is comparatively rare among children, this policy would still save 1,407 lives per year. Just under one third of all the boys who die in Britain each year would not die were childhood poverty eliminated. Perhaps most dramatic of all, in the areas of Britain where male childhood mortality rates are higher than the national average, *all* of the deaths above that average would be prevented. For girls this proportion is about a third. The effects are less dramatic for girls because fewer girls die and their geographical distribution of death in childhood is more even.

High rates of death among children (and infants in particular) are thus largely a tale of the effects of childhood poverty. Overall, five out of six of the child deaths over and above the national average would not occur were the poorest 20% of children to enjoy the life chances of the rest. Although the *number* of lives saved is not as high as those saved by adult-oriented policies, it is by ending childhood poverty that the greatest *proportional* improvement in inequalities in health can be made. The benefit is clearly enormous – so how might childhood poverty be eliminated?

Children do not live in isolation and in this report they have been ascribed a social class based on that of their parents. To alleviate *childhood* poverty requires the alleviation of *family* poverty by raising the living standards and material wealth of all people living in poverty who have children. It also requires raising the living standards of those who do not yet have children but who are poor – otherwise children continue to be born into poverty. Only a major redistribution of wealth and opportunity coupled with a great increase in the quality of services (especially education) could achieve this. Ending childhood poverty may be the most difficult goal to achieve, but it would have the greatest relative effect.

Targeting resources versus macroeconomics

The Prime Minister's constituency actually has a child mortality rate below the national average. Thus, for Sedgefield, the eradication of child poverty would make relatively little difference. There would be a slight fall in the number of boys dying per year (two lives saved), and virtually no change in the number of girls dying. Much larger impacts of this policy would be found in other parts of the country. This indicates quite well the way in which macroeconomic policy can have the greatest impact in places where the impact is most needed. The current government has experimented a great deal with trying to target resources through various kinds of 'zone' (health action zones, for example). This report shows that a better way to achieve widespread, large-scale results is to influence the whole of society through macroeconomic and social policy. The relationships between health and well being, and socioeconomic conditions are such that *those most in need will benefit most*.

The potential for reducing geographical inequalities in mortality

The report argues that the growth in geographical inequalities in health can be slowed or reduced if social policy is successful. The map (Figure 4) of 'lives saved' is testament to this. The map shows that all Britain would benefit from these policies, but that the greatest benefits would be concentrated in those areas which currently have the highest mortality rates. This suggests a *reduction* in the extent of geographical inequalities in death in Britain is very possible, not least because the rates of inequality are currently so high in historical terms. Reducing inequalities in health and helping those most in need turns out not to be theoritically difficult, nor to require complex zone-based approaches.

Summary

This chapter has shown how, in the past, changes in the meaning and equity of socioeconomic position have contributed to the growth and spatial pattern of inequalities in death in Britain. It then explained why social policy might reduce the geographical inequalities in health by estimating the number of premature deaths which could be avoided by the potential success of various government policies. The chapter shows how the lives saved would be concentrated in areas which currently have death rates higher than the national average.

- A mild redistribution of income would achieve the greatest number of lives saved across the country – 7,597 or 7% of all premature deaths which occur in Britain.
- The eradication of child poverty would have the greatest effect on those areas which currently have death rates higher than the national average – 92% of avoidable child deaths in those areas would be prevented.
- Attaining full employment would save 2,504 lives per year across Britain.
- Macroeconomic policies can be used to target areas most in need.
- These policies will have a much greater beneficial impact on men than on women. This is because a greater number of men die at ages below 65, and also because men appear to have been more likely to be affected (in health terms) by changes in their socioeconomic status.

Figure 4: Estimated number of lives saved by policy changes (ages <65)

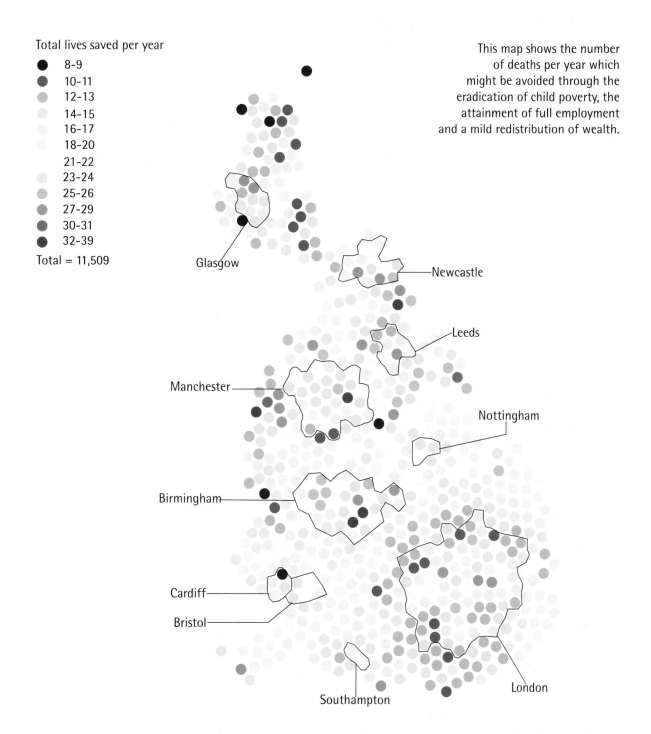

Total lives saved per year

- 8-9
- 10-11
- 12-13
- 14-15
- 16-17
- 18-20
- 21-22
- 23-24
- 25-26
- 27-29
- 30-31
- 32-39

Total = 11,509

This map shows the number of deaths per year which might be avoided through the eradication of child poverty, the attainment of full employment and a mild redistribution of wealth.

Glasgow
Newcastle
Leeds
Manchester
Nottingham
Birmingham
Cardiff
Bristol
Southampton
London

Note: These are lives saved only by the policy changes documented in the text, and only among the population aged 0-65.

3

How much of the change can be accounted for?

Aims

Chapter 2 exposed the size of the impact which social policy might have on health inequalities in the future. This chapter concentrates on the impact which policy-led social changes have had in the past. The chapter aims to answer three key questions:

- How much more (or less) of the variation in mortality rates across Britain can be accounted for in the early 1990s than in the early 1980s?
- Has social class and/or employment status become more or less important in accounting for the geographical variation in mortality rates?
- Is there a pattern to how much of the change in mortality rate variation can be accounted for?

Results

Figures 5 and 6 show the answers to questions 1 and 2. Figure 5 shows graphically and numerically the amount of variation in mortality across Britain which can be accounted for at each point in time. A figure of 100% would mean that all of the spatial variation in mortality under age 65 could be accounted for. In that case there would be no parts of the country in which more people died than would be expected or in which people lived longer than would be expected. In Figure 5 the results are presented graphically for four age/gender groups together with figures for the whole population. Results are presented for the whole of Britain (graphs on the left of the page), but also for just those constituencies in which the death rates are higher than the national average (graphs on the right). The differences

between these two sets of graphs will help to judge whether the influence of social class and employment is more important in less healthy areas.

Figure 5 shows that it is possible to account for a greater proportion of the variation in mortality across Britain in the early 1980s than in the early 1990s, although the change is not large. This is true for the population as a whole, for each of the age/gender groups within that total and for the areas with higher than average mortality. The 2% fall in explanation for Britain as a whole, from 84% to 82%, amounts to about an extra 11,000 deaths in the 1990s which these models cannot account for. These figures suggest that factors other than the age, gender, class and employment characteristics included in the model have become slightly more important in determining variation in mortality across Britain by the 1990s than they were in the 1980s. However, the fact that there has not been much change indicates that Britain's geography of mortality is still controlled, to a large degree, by the distribution of age, gender, social class and employment.

Figure 5 also shows that, in general terms, the models can account for a greater proportion of the mortality in those areas with death rates above the national average, most notably for the younger age group. This result suggests that influences on mortality are, perhaps, less complex in these areas, with social class and employment having the strongest influence.

Figure 5: How much spatial inequality can be accounted for in the 1980s and 1990s?

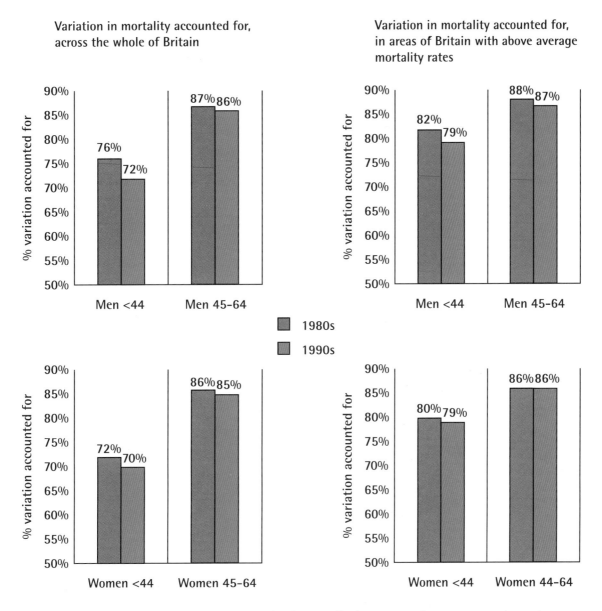

Variation in mortality accounted for, across the whole of Britain

Variation in mortality accounted for, in areas of Britain with above average mortality rates

The graphs show that the total amount of variation in mortality between parliamentary constituencies which can be accounted for by knowing about the age, gender, social class and employment status of constituents. For Britain as a whole, the figures are as follows:

The total amount of variation accounted for in the 1980s was 84% and in the 1990s it was 82%.

For those areas with higher than average mortality, the amount of variation explained was 86% in the 1980s and 84% in the 1990s.

Figure 6: How much of the geography of mortality can be accounted for by social class and unemployment in the 1980s and 1990s?

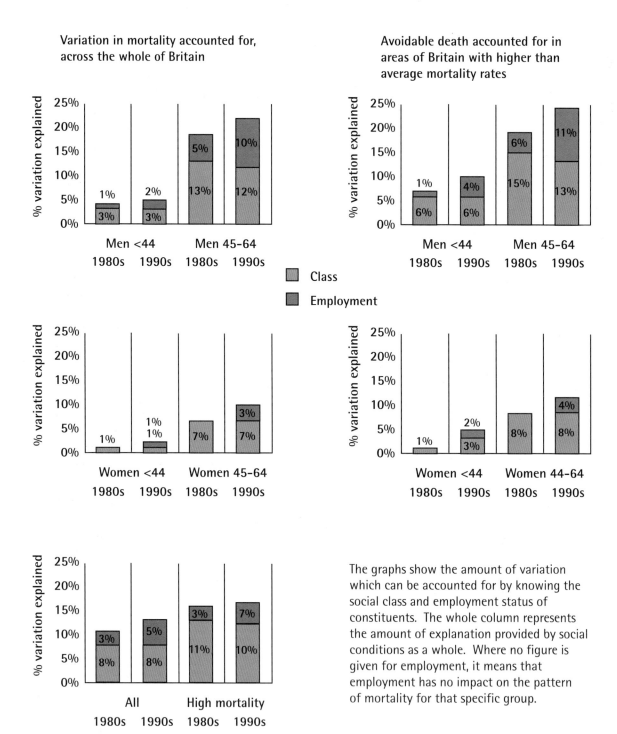

The graphs show the amount of variation which can be accounted for by knowing the social class and employment status of constituents. The whole column represents the amount of explanation provided by social conditions as a whole. Where no figure is given for employment, it means that employment has no impact on the pattern of mortality for that specific group.

Results in more detail

Class

In Figure 6 the graphs show how much of the variation which is left (after accounting for the different age and gender structures of constituencies) can be accounted for by including information about social class and employment status. Again, graphs are presented for different age and gender groups, and contrasted between Britain as a whole and areas in which mortality rates are higher than expected. There are considerable differences between these groups.

Taking the population as a whole (graph bottom left), it is clear that there has been little change either in Britain as a whole or in areas with higher mortality rates. Differences in the social class structure of constituencies explained about the same amount (8%) of the variation in mortality in the whole of Britain in the early 1990s as they did in the early 1980s. These results suggest that, contrary to popular beliefs, there has been little or no decline in the importance of social class in determining the patterns of mortality in Britain (Britain is certainly not becoming a classless society).

The results become slightly more complex when they are subdivided by age and gender. Notice that more of the variation for men can be accounted for by class than for women. It is difficult to say whether geographical inequalities in health for women are genuinely influenced less by their social class than those for men. Official statistics such as the Census (on which this report is based) tend to be very poor at accurately determining women's social class (and employment status). In general, women are more likely to move in and out of work more frequently than men, to work part-time and to have more than one job. All of those things make a one-off recording of occupation at the Census inadequate, and it is occupation which determines social class in these models. In addition, there have been dramatic changes in the nature of the labour market for women over the last 10-20 years and these are not well captured by the two Censuses on which these calculations are based. The model suggests that the influence of social class on the patterns of inequality for women has remained static.

For men aged 0-44 the importance of social class in explaining the pattern of mortality in Britain has not really changed, but there has been a very slight decline among the older group (45-64) both in areas of high mortality and in the country as a whole. For women aged 0-44, like men, class has not changed its influence and it remains very small in the country as a whole. In areas of higher than average mortality, class has increased its influence from 1% to 3%. Among the older women (45-64) class is very much more important. One reason for these changes may be that the later cohort of women all reached adulthood after the Second World War and experienced very different lives, on average, than those born a decade earlier.

Employment status

For the population as a whole, it is clear that in all of Britain, and especially in areas of high mortality, there has been a marked increase in the influence of employment (graph, bottom left). Again, notable differences between ages and genders are uncovered by looking at sub-groups.

For women of all ages, employment held almost no influence on their pattern of mortality in the 1980s, but by the 1990s it made an equal contribution to that of social class among younger women. For the older women, employment status has made a noteworthy contribution by the 1990s, especially in areas of above average mortality. For men there has been a very marked increase in the influence of employment – doubling for men of all ages, in the whole of Britain.

Social conditions as a whole

The graphs show that there has been a growth in the influence of social conditions on the patterns of inequality in mortality in Britain. Look at the combined influence of class and employment. Among the whole population, it has risen from 11% to 13% and, in areas of high mortality, from 14% to 17%. In these areas in particular, there has been a shift in the balance between social class and employment status in terms of which has the most potent influence on the patterns of mortality. In the early 1980s, class held by far the strongest influence, but by the 1990s their influences were becoming more comparable.

Among women in particular, the explanatory power of employment status has grown, whereas the explanatory power of women's social class has grown only for younger women in areas of higher mortality. Although employment status is still a smaller influence on geographical inequalities for women than for men, its importance has begun to be felt. This is likely to be reflecting the increased number of women in the formal labour market.

By the early 1990s then, class and employment status had grown greatly in importance. In general terms the amount of 'geography' of premature mortality which can be accounted for by age, gender, class and employment has fallen slightly over time. Within that which *can* be accounted for, socioeconomic position has become more important. The importance of age and gender for understanding the geography of mortality has fallen – the importance of socioeconomic status has risen.

The geography of change and explanation

Figures 1 and 3 show the changes which took place in the pattern of mortality and the extent to which these changes can be accounted for. A look at Figure 1 conveys two clear messages. First, there has been at least some change in the vast majority of the constituencies. Only 32 had relative rates of death in the early 1990s which were within 1% of those relative rates in the early 1980s. Second, the constituencies in which death rates have risen tend to be clustered together, most often in urban areas like Glasgow or London, while the areas in which the death rates have fallen tend to be more disparate and rural (with the notable exception of Leeds). Shettleston in Glasgow has the dubious distinction of being the constituency in which death rates became worse by the largest degree. The City of London and Westminster constituency appears to have fared best, reducing its death rates by the greatest amount.

Figure 3 shows a much starker geography and it is easy to see the North–South divide, with only central London upsetting the pattern. This is a map of how the changes in mortality rates which actually happened compare to those which were expected, given information about social and demographic change in the constituency populations. In general terms, the model leads us to expect more deaths in the South East of Britain (excluding London), and fewer in the North of England and in Scotland, than actually took place. Taking the population as a whole, in half of the constituencies it is possible to account for the changes in mortality rates to within 1% above or below the actual change. The model is also able to account for the changes to within 5% in 95% of the constituencies of Britain. However, some constituencies experienced changes which were beyond the model's ability to account for, and it is interesting to see which these are. Glasgow's Springburn, Shettleston, Pollok, Baillieston, and Maryhill and Manchester's Blackley are constituencies in which death rates rose or remained higher than can be accounted for here, to the greatest extent. Battersea, Bristol West, Kensington and Chelsea, Tooting, Edinburgh Central and Hammersmith and Fulham are those areas in which mortality rates fell or remained lower than this model can account for, to the greatest extent.

There are many plausible explanations as to why these constituencies are anomalous. Those in which death rates remained or became worse than expected are all poor inner city areas, experiencing continuing high levels of out-migration and faring particularly badly in economic terms over a very long period. The cumulative effects of deprivation are greater than those which can be measured at one point in time, but the models only focus on a snapshot of social conditions. Similarly the areas in which death rates became (or remained) lower than can be accounted for all tend to be already affluent or gentrifying areas and again the cumulative benefits of being so have not been well measured here.

It may well be that there is some factor peculiar to life in these areas which has an influence on people's risk of mortality over and above the effect of their own individual characteristics. These influences are called 'area effects' and may include factors such as local culture and elements of the physical and/or social environment. Further research would be required to account fully for these area effects, but it is clear that they are not random. Perhaps most importantly for this research, there are relatively few areas in which the model appears to have dramatically over- or underestimated the changes in mortality rates. Area effects are slight in most of Britain and only very strong in a few areas.

Figure 7: Variation in explanation for changing mortality rates (1983–93), differences by age and gender

Change not accounted for by class or employment

- 30–12% more death · All change explained
- 11–10% more death · 1–2% less death
- 9–7% more death · 3–4% less death
- 6–5% more death · 5–6% less death
- 4–3% more death • 7–8% less death
- 2–1% more death • 9–10% less death
- • 11–18% less death

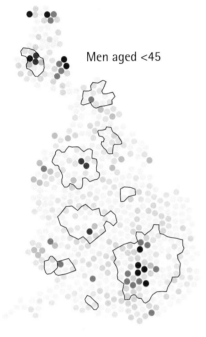

Men aged <45

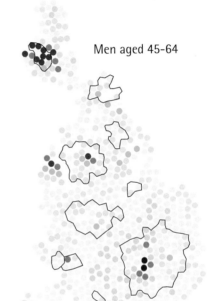

Men aged 45–64

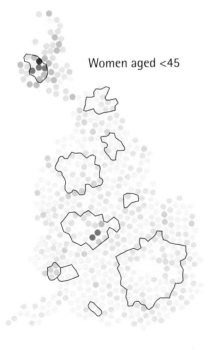

Women aged <45

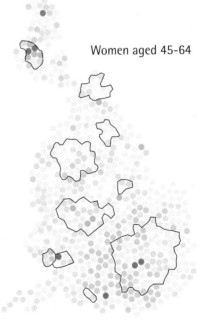

Women aged 45–64

Although it is important to examine this portrait of change and explanation for the whole population, of equal importance is the way in which the power of the models varies across the country among different age/gender groups. Figure 7 shows the same kind of information as that in Figure 3, but broken down by age and gender. In a sense, the four smaller maps 'sum' to that in Figure 3 and together the two figures answer question 3 (posed at the start of this chapter). Considering the younger men first (the map in the top left part of the page), a pattern quite similar to that for the whole population is evident, but notable for the higher number of English and Welsh constituencies at the extreme ends of the scale of explanation. The models have been more successful in accounting for the changes among Glasgow's younger men, and in fact have underestimated the very slight improvement in health in Glasgow Kelvin. West London seems to have fared substantially better than the models can explain. Among older men (although this group is still aged less than 65), the divide between urban North and South is seen most starkly. Men's health in Glasgow and Liverpool has become or remained very much worse than would be expected. For younger women (bottom left map), the models have performed best, but this is probably due to the fact that the geography of their life chances has changed least. Again, however, constituencies in Glasgow and Birmingham suffer much worse rates of premature mortality than the model expects. Among older women, the inexplicable changes adhere to a slightly stronger geographical pattern. Overall, analysis of the results by age and gender in this way reveals that the model is less able to explain the geography of mortality for men than for women and for the older people than the younger, but that there is not an enormous difference in model performance between these groups.

influence of these factors is stronger among those closer to 65, and stronger for men than women.

For the vast majority of the country, changes in the geography of demographic and socioeconomic structure appear to almost completely account for changes in the geography of premature mortality.

- A core set of areas remains (notably within Glasgow, Birmingham, and Liverpool) where the chances of premature mortality have remained or become inexplicably higher than the national average.
- The western fringes of London have enjoyed an inexplicable persistence of low or falling premature mortality rates.
- It may well be that influences on health which are peculiar to certain areas are at work here – these are called 'area effects'. Area effects are strongest in the places where mortality rates are highest or lowest.
- The large majority of geographical inequalities in health and their changes can be accounted for by the models of social change presented here.

In the next chapters, the modelling process is described in more detail.

Summary

In summary this chapter has shown that during the period from the early 1980s to the early 1990s, socioeconomic position has become much more important in determining the geography of premature mortality in Britain. It also suggests that employment status has become a more important feature in determining the power of socioeconomic position to explain changes in the geography of mortality. It appears that the

Principles and variables

This chapter outlines some of the concepts, principles and techniques used in the research. This, and subsequent chapters, adopt a step-by-step approach to explaining the concepts and methods employed to generate the results presented in Chapters 2 and 3. In order to detect and explain *changes* in the geographical pattern of mortality, it is important to understand how much of the pattern can be accounted for at *one point in time*. This process not only provides the foundations for an analysis of change, it will help to put any changes detected into context and introduce the reader to a set of important ideas, techniques and data. The questions addressed in this chapter are, 'why are people more likely to die prematurely in one area than another?', and 'how do we use that information to begin to account for the map of mortality?'.

Areas and maps

To explore how mortality varies from one area to another, there has to be a definition of 'area'. The 'areas' are the units into which Britain can be divided to show how mortality varies within it. In this report the area units are the parliamentary constituencies used in the 1997 general election. There are a number of reasons why constituencies make good units for this kind of work. First, constituencies are designed to contain a similar number of people so that we all have an equal opportunity to be represented by our Member of Parliament. On average a constituency contains about 88,000 people, although some constituencies are bigger than others. Having units of approximately the same population size means that the analysis does not unduly concentrate on small areas or ignore the varied experiences of people living in more populous areas. Second, constituencies contain enough

people to make the statistical analyses needed for a study like this robust and reliable. The study grouped people according to different combinations of age, gender, social class and employment status. Importantly, some groups are actually quite small (for example young unemployed professional women) and some groups have very low chances of mortality. Both factors mean that quite populous areas are needed to measure reliably the effects of social change on all groups in all areas. Third, constituencies are small enough to divide Britain into a mosaic of areas which can show patterns that are more complex than simple North–South or regional differences. The 641 constituencies represent a good compromise between the need for an area unit to contain enough people to make the findings meaningful, and not being so large that important variations within different regions of Britain are obscured. Lastly, parliamentary constituencies are geographical units which are meaningful, not only for the electorate who live in them, but for the Members of Parliament who represent them and who should safeguard their interests when formulating government policies.

While constituencies are fairly similar in terms of the number of people they contain, they vary greatly in terms of the physical size of the area they cover. Constituencies in inner London, where population density is high, cover only a small area of land in comparison with those in rural areas, which can be very large. If the mortality data for the 641 constituencies were mapped in a conventional way then it would be very difficult to see the detailed patterns of mortality in the inner cities (where mortality rates tend to be relatively high). Rural areas on the other hand (where mortality tends to be relatively low) would be very apparent and easily distinguishable. Mapping in a conventional way, where the space each constituency occupies on the page is directly proportional to its physical size, might lead to a distorted interpretation of the patterns of mortality. For this reason cartograms are used to present the results of this report (see Figure 2 for more information).

Data and variables used

Premature mortality

Throughout the report, deaths which have occurred among people under the age of 65 are referred to as *premature*. It is geographical patterns and trends in the mortality of this group which the report aims to account for. Although 65 is conventionally the age which marks a premature death from any other, the fact that average life expectancy for all Britain's population is well above 65 means that the results presented here are conservative. Were this report to have treated any death before the average life expectancy as premature, the results would have been very much more extreme in terms of the absolute numbers of deaths being reported.

Age and gender

When explaining patterns in the mortality of a population, an important factor to consider is its composition in terms of age structure and the relative numbers of men and women. Obviously, the older a person is, the more likely they are to die. Those most at risk of a premature death are aged closest to 65. There are also clear differences in the life chances of men and women. Men and women have different chances of death at all stages of their lives and death rates are generally higher for men than women. It is therefore important that the number of men and women of each age in a constituency is known. Five-year age groups are generally sufficient to take this into account, and those are the categories used here. This means that, for example, rather than knowing precisely how many men aged 20, 21, 22, 23 and 24 there are in a constituency, it is sufficient to know the number of men aged between 20 and 24. However, we also separately identify those aged 0 from ages 1-4, to allow for the expected higher rates of mortality in the first 12 months of life.

Age–gender SMRs

Figure 8 maps mortality for constituencies in Britain in 1991-95, using a cartogram. The shading represents the actual total number of deaths, for both men and women aged less than 65, which occurred in that five-year period. The constituencies shaded from light blue to indigo have fewer total deaths than average, whereas those shaded from orange to red have higher actual numbers of deaths. Many constituencies have actual numbers of death that are in the middle of the range.

Figure 8 does not take into account the slightly different sizes of the populations in different areas, nor their age-gender structure. Age-gender SMRs are calculated for each constituency, to take these differences into account. As touched on in Chapter 1, SMRs are a measure of the population's chance of dying each year, relative to the national average. They allow the mortality rates in different areas with different population sizes and compositions to be directly compared. An SMR below 100 indicates that the area has mortality which is relatively low compared to the national average, whereas areas with SMRs greater than 100 have relatively high mortality. An SMR of 200, for example, would mean that the population experienced mortality at rates twice that which was normal for the nation as a whole. An SMR of 50 would mean that the population experienced mortality at rates half that of the national average. In this report, to maintain comparability with official figures, we use the England and Wales average as the 'national average' for each time period. Figure 9 shows SMRs for constituencies, again for deaths in the period 1991-95. The areas shaded indigo have the lowest mortality, with SMRs between 60 and 70. The areas shaded red have the highest SMRs, between 170 and 228. A North–South divide is clearly apparent with a swathe of blue visible across the South, although London has some higher rates. This map of SMRs shows a more extreme geography of mortality than the map of the actual number of deaths.

Figure 8: Numbers of deaths (1991–95)

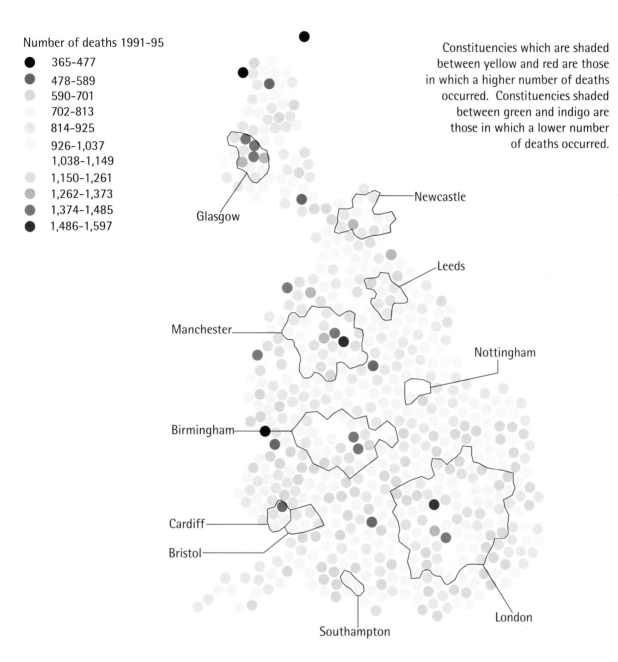

Number of deaths 1991–95
- 365–477
- 478–589
- 590–701
- 702–813
- 814–925
- 926–1,037
- 1,038–1,149
- 1,150–1,261
- 1,262–1,373
- 1,374–1,485
- 1,486–1,597

Constituencies which are shaded between yellow and red are those in which a higher number of deaths occurred. Constituencies shaded between green and indigo are those in which a lower number of deaths occurred.

Glasgow

Newcastle

Leeds

Manchester

Nottingham

Birmingham

Cardiff

Bristol

London

Southampton

Figure 9: Standardised mortality ratio (ages <65) (1991–95)

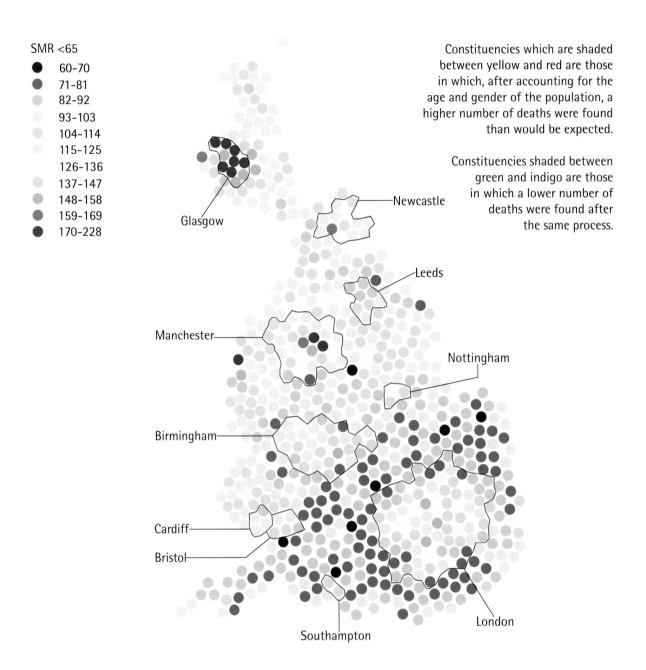

SMR <65

- 60–70
- 71–81
- 82–92
- 93–103
- 104–114
- 115–125
- 126–136
- 137–147
- 148–158
- 159–169
- 170–228

Constituencies which are shaded between yellow and red are those in which, after accounting for the age and gender of the population, a higher number of deaths were found than would be expected.

Constituencies shaded between green and indigo are those in which a lower number of deaths were found after the same process.

Glasgow

Newcastle

Leeds

Manchester

Nottingham

Birmingham

Cardiff

Bristol

Southampton

London

England and Wales SMR = 100

Social class

After taking into account the age and gender structure of a constituency, the next factor to take into account is the social class of the resident population. Differences in life chances for different social classes have been apparent since such analyses were first possible and they are among the largest between groups of any definition. There are a number of measures of a person's class which could be used, including income or occupation. The UK Census was the only data source which could provide any measures of social class for every constituency in Britain at two points in time and the best class measure in the Census is based on occupation.

The Census social class classification uses six social class groups. The box below shows the type of occupations which are categorised into these six groups. However, this measure is not just an indicator of the type of job that people do. A social class is also indicative of many other factors which are a measure of a person's relative standing in life – their income, wealth and educational qualifications, for example. The concept of social class is also important in that while it indicates a person's current relative position, it is also indicative of their journey through life. The social class of a child's parents will affect the area in which they can afford and choose to live, the school that they attend and their child's peer group. These things affect educational outcomes and the individual's own social class in adulthood. Social class is also important in the way that it relates to how people behave in their day-to-day lives. The concept, practice and process of social class pervade almost all aspects of life in Britain today.

Class stratification is clearly apparent in the risk of death and there is a distinct social class gradient

Table 6: Total expectation of life by social class (ONS Longitudinal Study) for men and women, England and Wales (1992–96)

Social class	Men	Women
I	77.7	83.4
II	75.8	81.1
IIIN	75.0	80.4
IIIM	73.5	78.8
IV	72.6	77.7
V	68.2	77.0
Difference I-V	9.5	6.4
All	73.9 yrs	79.2 yrs

Source: Hattersley (1999)

Registrar General's social class (based on occupation)

Social class	Occupation type
I	Professional (such as, accountants, electronic engineers)
II	Managerial and technical/intermediate (such as, proprietors and managers - sales, production, works and maintenance managers)
IIIN	Skilled non-manual (such as, clerks and cashiers - not retail)
IIIM	Skilled manual (such as, drivers of road goods vehicles, metal working production fitters)
IV	Partly skilled manual (such as, storekeepers and warehousemen, machine tool operators)
V	Unskilled manual (such as, building and civil engineering labourers, cleaners etc)

Source: Bunting (1997)

in mortality rates for both men and women. The most recent evidence shows that the total size of the social class (I-V) mortality gap is 9.5 years for men and 6.4 years for women (see Table 6). The health effect of social class accumulates over a person's lifetime and this reiterates the assertion above that social class is far more of a process than a category into which each person might be placed by virtue of their job title.

The analyses in this report rely on Census data to indicate people's social class. Since the Census is simply a snapshot in time it has not been possible to take account of an individual's changing social position through life. It is also the case that not everyone is assigned to a social class in the Census because it designates class through occupation. This means that children and people over retirement age are not 'issued' a social class as part of the Census process. However, while the circumstances of some people might disqualify them from certain categories on the census form, no one lives in a vacuum outside social class structure; they are as much part of it as those who qualify for a class label through the Census form.

Since social class has such an impact on health, and we are trying to understand the map of mortality in Britain, it is important to know the social class position of everyone in each constituency – not just those who qualify through the Census form. We have therefore devised a mechanism for assigning children, adults not in work and older people to an appropriate social class and this is described briefly in Chapter 6 and in detail in the technical report.

Unemployment

Unemployment is another important factor which affects life chances but it should not be thought of as equivalent to being at the bottom of the social class scale – unemployment is more complex than that. First, it can affect individuals who work in any occupation, although some occupations and classes are much more prone to unemployment than others. Unemployment can also affect individuals for relatively short periods of time, having a minimal impact on a person's standard of living (for example, they may be moving between jobs and have savings to draw on). However, it can also last for many months or years and in that instance have a much greater affect on a person's standard of living and eventually their health.

Second, the chances of being unemployed are also strongly area-based. Areas which rely on declining industries are particularly vulnerable to unemployment and prone to the effects of broader changes in the national labour market and international economy.

The health effects of unemployment

The impact of unemployment on health is well established. An effect is found even when social class and behavioural factors (such as smoking) have been taken into account. For example, a study of over 6,000 men aged 40-59 over a five-year period found that those who had been unemployed at some point in those five years were twice as likely to have died than those who had been continuously employed (Morris et al, 1994). Long-term unemployment is especially damaging. It runs down a person's resources, not only in financial terms but also socially and mentally. In this way, the health effects of unemployment, rather like the effects of low socioeconomic position, accumulate over time.

Unemployment is not the only alternative to being employed. People can also be *economically inactive*, which includes those too sick to work (and anyone not officially in or seeking work). Economic inactivity also carries a much higher risk of mortality than being in regular employment. The models in this report take account of those who are economically inactive as well as the unemployed which is why we refer to 'employment status' rather than just 'unemployment' in this text.

If employment status affects the chances of death, and the chances of being unemployed or economically inactive are higher for some types of people than others – and in some types of areas than others – it is important to take employment status into account when attempting to explain the geography of mortality in Britain.

Interaction effects

The four factors that are used in this report to account for geographical patterns in mortality are thus the *age* and *gender* structure of the population of an area, and its composition in terms of *social class* and *employment status*. As has been explained, these four factors are each related to life chances, but they are also related to each other. For instance, those who work in manual occupations are more likely to be unemployed, those in social classes I and II tend to be older, there are more men than women in social classes I and II, and so on. For this reason, it is important to know the number of people in each constituency with each possible combination of characteristics. Only then could the effects of each characteristic be separately identified. Chapter 6 explains how that requirement was met.

Summary

In this chapter the relationship between age, gender, social class, employment status and health has been briefly explained. It should now be clear that the combination of these characteristics which an individual has, affects their chances of premature mortality. We can see these relationships at a national level – they combine to produce the *national average* death rate. It is hopefully not difficult to see that if a particular constituency contains a high number of people with characteristics which place them at higher risk of dying, we would expect that constituency to have a higher number of deaths.

The chapter made these points:

- Parliamentary constituencies are sensible areal units with which to study the geography of mortality in Britain.
- They need to be mapped using cartograms to visualise the geography properly.
- Mortality rates are affected by age, gender, social class and employment status.
- These characteristics are related to each other very strongly.
- The composition of constituencies, in respect of age, gender, social class and employment status varies. There is a strong geography to social class and employment.
- It is important to have detailed information about the numbers of people with each possible combination of these characteristics if they are to be used to model mortality rates.

In the next chapter, temporal changes in the way Britain's population is made up are explored, together with changes in the distribution of different kinds of people across the country.

How British society is changing

In the previous chapter, the relationships between age, gender, class, employment status and risk of premature death were explored. It was explained that differing combinations of these characteristics were related to people's chances of death and that therefore the profile of a constituency population, in terms of the numbers of people with each combination of these characteristics, would be related to the numbers of deaths which occurred there. To understand changes in the geography of mortality it is therefore necessary to look first at how the geography of these four factors has changed.

In the report we have projected forward the population recorded in the 1981 and 1991 Censuses so that the data refer to the mid-points of the two five-year periods being studied. Thus, the populations to which we refer are those in 1983 and 1993.

Age and gender

First, the population pyramids in Figures 10 and 11 show the age–gender structure of the population for the two time periods 1983 and 1993. They show the proportion of the population in each five-year age group, with the bars on the right referring to men and those on the left referring to women. It is the similarities rather than the differences which are most remarkable when comparing these two distributions – there is little change in the age–gender structure of the *total* population between the early 1980s and the early 1990s. For individual constituencies, however, there may be a greater degree of change, perhaps as (younger) people move in and out of areas in search of work, or as they move into education as universities take more students. These changes and their impact on the numbers of deaths in each constituency are taken into account by our methods.

Social class

The proportion of people in the different social classes for the same years can be seen in Figure 12. For women, in 1983 the largest social class group was skilled non-manual workers (IIIN), and over half of all women were classified as being in non-manual occupations (I + II + IIIN = 55%). By 1993 this proportion had expanded to 58% of women being in non-manual jobs, mostly due to an increase in the proportion of women in social class II and a decrease in social class IV. Note that at both time points only 3% of women are in the highest social class group.

For men, there has been a rise in the proportion allocated to social class I – 6% in 1983 and 7% in 1993 – however, the majority of men are still classed in manual occupations. The overall proportion in non-manual occupations has risen – from 42% in 1983 to 46% in 1993. This change is accounted for mostly by an increase in social class II and a decrease in social class IIIM. Class IIIM was the dominant social class of the mostly male occupations which were lost in Britain over this period due to deindustrialisation. A typical IIIM occupation would be coal mining.

It is not only the relative size of social classes which change over time. The chances of death associated with belonging to each class alters too, as Table 7 shows. To account for the changing patterns of mortality in Britain it is necessary not only to know how the population in each area is changing but also to know the changing importance (in terms of health) of belonging to any particular age/gender/class/employment group.

Figure 10: Population by age and gender (1983)

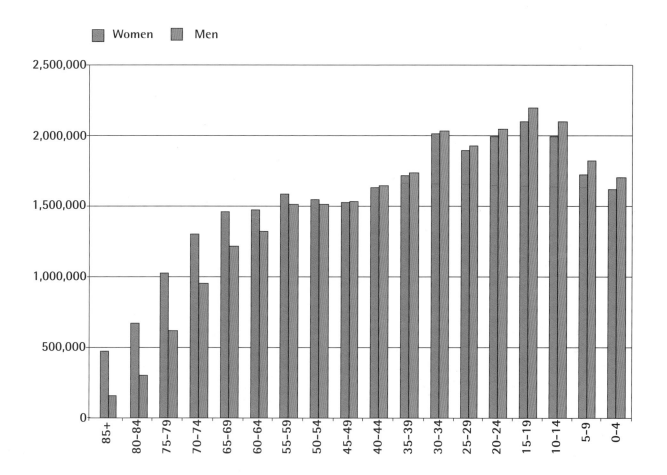

Figure 11: Population by age and gender (1993)

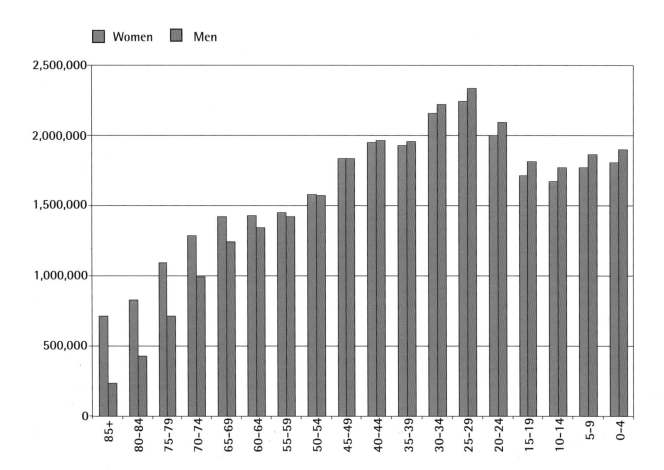

Figure 12: Change in occupational class structure (1983–93)

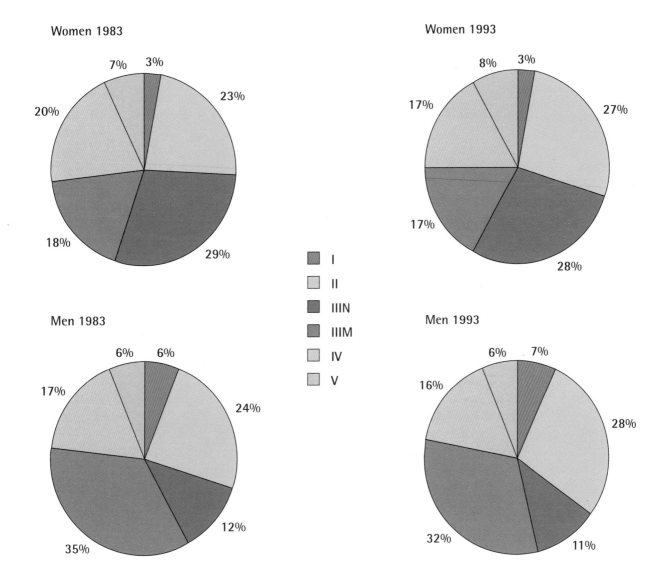

Women 1983

Women 1993

Men 1983

Men 1993

Legend:
- I
- II
- IIIN
- IIIM
- IV
- V

These pie charts show the changes in occupational class structure which took place between 1983 and 1993, for men and women of all ages. Notice the growth in the proportion of women in classes II and V and the growth in I and II for men. Notice too, the much higher proportion of men in class I as compared to women, at both points in time. In these pie charts, everyone has an occupational class, whether they are employed, unemployed or retired.

Table 7: SMRs by social class, men aged 15/20-64, England and Wales (1920s-1990s)

Year	I	II	III		IV	V	Ratio V:I
			IIIN	IIIM			
1921-23	82	94	95		101	125	1.52
1930-32	90	94	97		102	111	1.23
1949-53	86	92	101		104	118	1.37
1959-63	76	81	100		103	143	1.88
1970-72	77	81	99	106	114	137	1.78
1979-80/1982-83	66	76	94	106	116	165	2.50
1991-93	66	72	100	117	116	189	2.86

Note: For 1921-23, 1930-32, 1949-53, 1959-63 and 1970-72 men aged 15-64 are included. For 1979-80/1982-83 and 1991-93 men aged 20-64 are included.

Source: 1921-23, 1930-32, 1949-53 and 1959-63 from Thompson (1975); 1970-72 and 1979-80/1982-83 from Blaxter (1991); 1991-93 from Drever (1997)

The 'ratio' column in Table 7 measures the health gap between the highest and lowest social class over time. This gap is getting wider – not because the age–gender profile of each class is changing (as shown by the pie charts), but because there is a growing and real difference between the life chances, wealth and opportunities enjoyed by different classes. The table suggests that the *effect* of social class on the chances of dying has become more potent over time. If the relationship between social class and premature mortality has grown stronger, and we know that the distribution of the population belonging to each class has also changed, it is vital to include class in any analysis of the changing *geography* of mortality.

Unemployment

Figure 13 shows the average number of unemployed people (men and women) during the period 1971-93. This shows that unemployment was relatively high in constituencies located in Glasgow, Newcastle and surrounding areas, Manchester, Birmingham and London, with a cluster of particularly high numbers of unemployed people living in and around Liverpool. Conversely, few people are unemployed in the South of England and in the areas surrounding London.

Figure 14 shows change in the average chances of being unemployed between 1971 and 1983, and between 1981 and 1993. Together, the two maps show that many of the areas which already had high counts of unemployment have experienced increases in unemployment between the 1980s and 1990s (much of this increase occurred in the years 1980-83). The estimate of the effect of unemployment in 1983 and 1993 used here is based on average rates of unemployment over a 12-year period (1971-83 and 1981-93). Using rates for any one particular year would not be representative of the employment history of an area. The rates used here are corrected to allow for the distortions in the official claimant count of unemployment which occur through time.

Since this report explores the effect of socioeconomic changes over time on changes in the patterns of mortality, it is also important to consider possible changes in the relationship between unemployment and health. A study based in Finland found that the association between mortality and unemployment weakened as the general unemployment rate increased. When unemployment was low it was found that the mortality rates among the unemployed were about twice as high for men and about 1.5 times higher for women compared to those for the employed. However, at a time of high unemployment, these ratios were lower, at about 1.3 times as high for both men and women

Figure 13: Long-term unemployment, average number of people unemployed per year (1971–93)

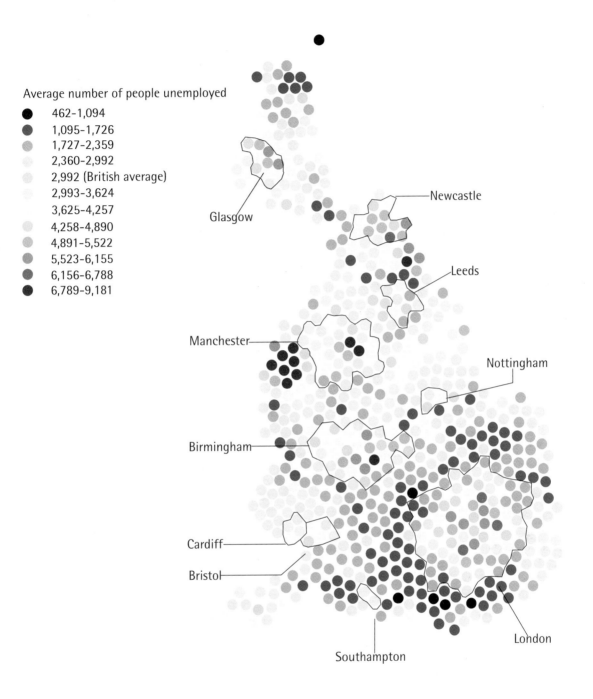

Average number of people unemployed

- 462–1,094
- 1,095–1,726
- 1,727–2,359
- 2,360–2,992
- 2,992 (British average)
- 2,993–3,624
- 3,625–4,257
- 4,258–4,890
- 4,891–5,522
- 5,523–6,155
- 6,156–6,788
- 6,789–9,181

Glasgow

Newcastle

Leeds

Manchester

Nottingham

Birmingham

Cardiff

Bristol

Southampton

London

Figure 14: Change in long-term unemployment rates (1983-93), 16-64 year olds. long-term unemployed

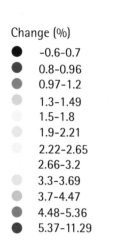

Change (%)
● -0.6-0.7
● 0.8-0.96
● 0.97-1.2
○ 1.3-1.49
○ 1.5-1.8
○ 1.9-2.21
○ 2.22-2.65
  2.66-3.2
○ 3.3-3.69
○ 3.7-4.47
● 4.48-5.36
● 5.37-11.29

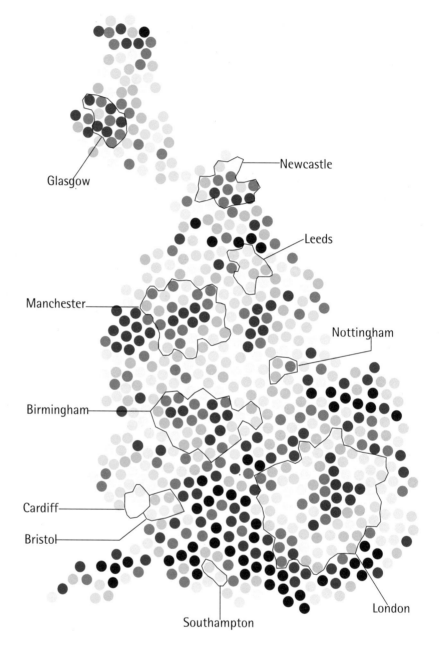

Change is measured by
the difference in the
percentage of the 16-64
year olds employed at
each point in time. If the
unemployment rate was
7% in 1983 and 9% in
1993, the change is +2%.

Table 8: Mortality rates of men of working age by economic activity at the 1971 and 1981 Censuses (1971 and 1981 Longitudinal Study cohorts), England and Wales

Economic activity	Rates per 100,000 people	
	1971–79	**1981–89**
Employed	302	227
Unemployed*	410	319
Death rate ratio	1.36	1.41

Note: * For both these time periods unemployment was defined as seeking work or waiting to take up a job in the week preceding the Census.

Source: Bethune (1997)

(Martikainen and Valkonen, 1996). This might suggest that as unemployment becomes more common, the impact on health is reduced (perhaps it is no longer such a stigma). However, this does not seem to be the case for England and Wales, as Table 8 suggests.

In Britain the health effect of unemployment seems to have become more potent, rather than less. Potency is measured by the ratio between the two rates (shown in the table). In the report, however, a conservative assumption is made that the detrimental effect of unemployment on health is stable over time. Thus the increase in the importance of employment reported in Chapter 3 has to be due to the rising number and geographical concentration of unemployed and economically inactive people in Britain.

Summary

Many of the factors which might influence the geography of mortality in Britain are changing. However, this does not mean that the changes cannot be monitored and measured when attempting to account for the changing pattern of mortality in Britain. To recap, here are the factors which have changed in Britain between the 1980s and 1990s which have to be measured before it is possible to analyse accurately the patterns of mortality.

- The numbers of people of each age and gender living in each area.
- The proportion of these groups belonging to each social class.
- The distribution of unemployment by age, gender, area and class.
- Changes in the risk of death for groups with all possible combinations of age, gender, class and employment status.
- Although all of the information needed is available in some format; many corrections and adjustments are necessary to bring the data up to the highest possible standard.

As described in Chapter 4, it is important to have detailed information about the numbers of people with each possible combination of these characteristics. This information is not directly provided by official statistics, but the components needed to create the necessary data are. The next chapter explains how such figures can be estimated given only limited information.

6

Methods and measurements

This chapter is a detailed description of the data and methods employed in this research. In Chapter 4, relationships between individual characteristics and the chances of death were explored and described. Chapter 5 illustrated how the changing geographical distribution of the population, the groups within it and their chances of dying, could be measured. This chapter describes how knowledge about those relationships has been combined with other data about the British population to analyse changes in the variation of mortality rates across the country – in short, how the maps in Figures 1 and 3 were actually produced. The methods are described in brief here but a comprehensive description and explanation is provided in the technical report (available free at www.social-medicine.com).

Actual deaths versus expected deaths

The key to this entire report is the relationship between the actual number of deaths which occurred in a parliamentary constituency and the number which were expected to occur, where that expectation was based on knowing about the types and numbers of people who live there. As explained in Chapter 4, the analysis was based on four characteristics through which any individual might be described: age, gender, social class and employment status. As was also explained in Chapter 4, there is a clear relationship between the possession of specific combinations of these four characteristics and a person's chances of dying in any year. Chapter 5 showed that it is possible to estimate how the numbers of people in possession of these characteristics change in each place and how the influence of their characteristics also changes over time. The method employed in this report is simple – if the number of people with a specific set of characteristics is known, and the chance of that category of person dying in a year is also known, an estimate of how many of those people are expected to die in a year can be made.

If, for example, the (national) average chance of a man dying aged between 45 and 49, in social class V and unemployed was, say, 1 in 100 in a particular year, and there are 500 men of that age, class and employment status living in a constituency, we would expect five of them to die in a typical year – five is the expected number of deaths. If, in fact, five of the 500 men with those characteristics really did die in a given year, the actual number of deaths is the same as the expected and all of the deaths among that group can be considered to have been accounted for. If, for example, 10 of the 500 men died, the actual number of deaths exceeds the expected number and indicates that the death rate for this group, in this area, is higher than the national average. If the actual number of deaths was two, it would indicate that the death rate, for this group in this area, is lower than the national average.

All the results given in this report are derived from the same kind of simple calculation. Unfortunately, however, obtaining the data needed to make these calculations was not as straightforward. Most of the work undertaken for this report involved the manipulation of data which are publicly available into a format which would allow the calculations. The rest of this chapter briefly describes the raw data utilised and the techniques employed to facilitate the calculations.

Acquiring the data

As can be seen from the example above, there are three elements to the calculation. First, the number of people with the specific set of characteristics is needed (in the example, it was 500). Second, the chances of death over a period of time for that particular group are needed (this is more often known as the rate). Finally, the actual number of deaths for that group is needed. This last item of data was by far the most straightforward to obtain, so it will be described first.

The Office for National Statistics (ONS) provides some limited details about every death registered in England and Wales, with similar data available for Scotland from the General Register Office (Scotland). From these records a count was produced of the deaths which took place in each parliamentary constituency in the early 1980s and the early 1990s, grouped by five-year age bands for men and for women (with children aged under 1 as a separate category). It is standard practice to measure the number of deaths which took place for populations of constituency size over a five-year period, rather than in one year. This is to prevent a distortion of the mortality rates which can be caused by unusual events, such as a 'flu outbreak. That kind of event might cause a higher number of deaths than normal among vulnerable people, or in particular areas, which could distort the results. Counts of deaths in this format constituted the actual deaths data.

Obtaining counts of the number of people, with each combination of the individual characteristics, for every parliamentary constituency at the two points in time was more complex. Although the Census provides data on the numbers of people in each age group, in each possible employment status and, to an extent, in each social class, these figures are merely totals for each category of each characteristic. Thus, the Census tells us how many men aged 45-49 there were in a constituency in 1991, and how many unemployed men there were; it also tells us how many men aged 45-49 were unemployed, but it does not tell us how many of those were in each social class. In addition to that difficulty, as discussed in Chapter 4, the Census does not record a social class for everyone (notably the retired population, adults who have not worked for 10 years, and children aged under 16 years old). In simple terms, the Census provided enough raw

components to build the data set needed, but a great deal of manipulation was required. The process is described in detail in the technical report, and in brief below.

There were three key manipulations made to the data which are summarised in Table 9.

Although each manipulation is apparently quite straightforward in theory, in practice carrying them out for every constituency in Britain at two points in time was a complex task. Computer programmes were written and it is estimated that about 0.3 billion calculations took place to achieve these results. The end result was the main data set required for the research. The remaining data set needed was that describing the rates of death for groups with different combinations of characteristics.

Death rates for groups described by their age, gender and social class were obtained from the ONS Longitudinal Study (LS). This is a special data set which stems from the Census, but which provides information about a small sample of English and Welsh people in much greater detail than do the conventional Census data. The Census records are linked to the government's death records which allows calculation of death rates for quite specific groups of people, including those described by their age, gender and social class. Death rates distinguishing between those employed, unemployed and economically inactive among each group were estimated by combining published information on the effects of employment status with the rates from the ONS. A thorough explanation of the method is provided in the technical report. These death rates all referred to the combined English and Welsh populations, and we know that death rates in Scotland (as a whole) are slightly higher among some groups. However, the data set assembled here was the best possible since there is no comparable longitudinal data set for Scotland from which to derive appropriate death rates at the level of detail required. The best option available was to utilise rates based on the English and Welsh and remain aware of the potential consequences for the results. In fact, the effect of doing this will be to make all the findings for Scotland very slightly conservative. It is important to understand that the mortality rate for each group is the *average* for England and Wales together and that this has been presented here as the 'national' average.

Table 9: Key manipulations to the data

	Manipulation 1	Manipulation 2	Manipulation 3
What was it?	Estimate the number of people falling into each possible combination of individual characteristics (eg how many men aged 45-49 in class V and unemployed were there in this constituency?).	Assign an appropriate social class to those people who do not receive one in the UK Census (eg the retired, children, people who had never worked or had not worked for the last 10 years).	Project the data forward so that they estimate the population characteristics of 1983 and 1993 rather than 1981 and 1991 as the study is of deaths in the five years around these mid-points.
Why was it needed?	Death rates differ significantly between groups, even where just one characteristic is different (eg the death rate for men, aged 40-45, in class I who are employed is significantly lower than that for men of the same age and class who are unemployed).	No one is isolated from the effects of their social position. The way in which the Census treats social class differs from the 'real world'. This manipulation squeezed extra value from the Census data to try and make it more represent-ative of how life really is.	Adhering to convention, the method used deaths occurring in a five-year period at each point in time (1981-85, 1991-95). The population data needed to refer to an appropriate mid-point in the five years (1983, 1993) and to be corrected for under-enumeration.
How was it carried out?	A technique called Iterative Proportional Fitting was employed. This takes the information which is known and uses it to make the best possible estimate of that which is not. The information which is not known – the detailed counts of particular groups – is estimated so that it both sums to the correct marginal total in an area and that it replicates, as best as possible, the known national and regional distributions.	Those who do not have a class in the Census are assigned one based on other people of the same age and gender who live in the same neighbourhood (ward) (eg if, according to the Census, 25% of men aged 20-24 are in class IIIM, 25% of men aged 20-24 who were not given a class by the Census will be given class IIIM).	By assuming that changes to the constituency population which took place between 1981 and 1991 happened evenly (ie at the same rate every year), two years' worth of change could be applied to the 1981 Census data to produce population estimates for 1983. A similar process was applied to 1991 data, using estimates of the population in 1996 to describe a typical year's worth of change.

Using the data and getting results

Following the work described above, the data were now assembled and ready to be analysed. All the analyses were based on the relationship between the actual number of deaths in a constituency and the number expected. Perhaps the best way to explain how the results were obtained is to use a worked example. Here, the analysis will be demonstrated for men in Sedgefield, Tony Blair's constituency. The results for the early 1990s are as follows:

Step 1: Actual number of deaths

The actual number of deaths amongst men in Sedgefield, aged under 65, for the five years between 1991 and 1995 was 630 (that is, an average of 126 per year).

Step 2: The first expected number

The first calculation produced an expected number of deaths for Sedgefield's men, aged less than 65, based just on their age structure. Table 10 explains the calculation.

Table 10: Characteristics of men aged <65 in the constituency of Sedgefield (1991–95)

Age group	0	1–4	5–9	10–14	15–19	20–24	25–29	30–34	35–39	40–44	45–49	50–54	55–59	60–64	Total
Number of men of that age in 1993															
	574	2,199	2,866	2,879	2,726	2,809	3,251	3,049	2,903	3,151	3,102	2,617	2,345	2,181	36,652

Number in each group multiplied by national average risk of death
over five years based on age and gender, to give:

Expected number of deaths in that group															
	20	4	2	3	8	12	14	15	19	30	50	71	111	181	540
Actual number of deaths (five yrs)															
	13	2	1	4	6	16	3	15	22	36	44	100	142	226	630
SMR															117

The number of men in each age group was known and was multiplied by the national average death rate to get an expected number of deaths for the five-year period for each group. Expected deaths were then totalled and that number was compared to the actual number which occurred. So, in Sedgefield in the early 1990s (1991-95) there were actually 630 deaths among men aged under 65 but, using the national average death rates and the numbers of men in each age group, only 540 were 'expected'. The SMR for Sedgefield's men, aged less than 65, is given by dividing 630 by 540 and multiplying by 100, making 117. In simple terms, men under 65 in Sedgefield have a 17% higher chance of dying than the national average.

Step 3: Adding social class to the model

To include information about the social class composition of Sedgefield's men, the process was almost exactly the same as before, but the number of groups was increased so that there was one for every possible combination of age and social class. For example, Sedgefield's 3,049 30-34 year old men are made up of 153 in class I, 718 in class II, 231 in class IIIN, 1,221 in class IIIM, 602 in class IV and 123 in class V. A slightly different death rate was applied to each of these groups because, on average, the risk of death increases with lower social class. Otherwise, the process was exactly the same as before, and of course the *actual* number of deaths was the same. When class information was added to the model, the

expected number of deaths rose to 551. This is because the calculation was better able to take account of the higher death rates among Sedgefield men due to relatively high numbers of them being working class. The SMR (adjusted for class) now came down to 114.

Step 4: Adding employment status to the model

To include information about employment status, the number of groups was increased again so that there was one for every possible combination of age, social class and employment status. A slightly different death rate was applied to each group, reflecting the fact that the national average death rate is higher for the unemployed than the employed – regardless of social class (although interacting with it somewhat). The difference in mortality rates between the employed and unemployed varies with social class and age. When employment status information was added to the model for Sedgefield's men aged under 65, the expected number of deaths rose to 581, making an SMR (adjusted for class and employment) of 108. This means that even after allowing for the employment and class structure of this population, their chances of death are still 8% higher than the national average. On the other hand, without the information about class and employment status, those chances of death would appear to be 17% higher – a substantial amount of the apparently high death rate has been 'accounted for' by understanding the class and employment characteristics of Sedgefield's

Table 11: Accounting for changes in men's mortality in Sedgefield (1980s to 1990s)

	1980s	1990s	Change
SMR based on age and gender	120	117	-3
SMR based on age, gender and social class	117	114	-3
SMR based on age, gender, social class and employment status	113	108	-5
Amount accounted for by social class	3	3	0
Amount accounted for by social class and employment status	7	9	+2

men. The first rate (17% higher than the national average) is not excused or justified – the results mean that most of that excess is due to the inequalities which persist between differing social classes and between those in and out of work.

The maps in Figure 15 show, for the early 1990s, the geographical pattern in the power of social class and employment status in accounting for the map of mortality across Britain. They are essentially maps showing how the importance of socioeconomic position for explaining death varied across the country at that time. They show, in summary form, the statistics which have been described in detail for Sedgefield for every constituency in Britain. (Appendix A provides these data for every constituency in Britain.)

All the data needed to track changes in the pattern of mortality in Britain over time, and to explore changes in the power of social class and employment status stemmed from the same kind of calculation. SMRs can be produced in the same way for the early 1980s, providing six figures to assess and compare. Table 11 provides these figures for Sedgefield.

As can be seen from these figures, there was a slight fall in the relative (to the national average) mortality rates for men in Sedgefield aged less than 65, between the early 1980s and the early 1990s, though they remain uncomfortably high. When social class and employment status are taken into account, the SMR has fallen more substantially. This means that socioeconomic position has become *more* important in determining Sedgefield's mortality rates during the decade in question. Interestingly, the power of social class to explain the constituency's mortality rate has remained static, but the strength of employment status has risen. This reflects a rise

in the importance of unemployment in determining the constituency's health.

This style of analysis forms the basis for the report and shows how the social class and employment status of a constituency's population has become more (or less) important in determining its mortality rates and thus its part in forming a geography of mortality across the country. In the rest of this chapter, the method is reviewed in a critical light, sources of error are discussed and the robustness of the results is considered.

Error and model testing

It is important to consider the potential sources of error in the work and how they might influence the results. The potential sources of error can be loosely divided into two groups with the first referring to the accuracy of the estimates of numbers in each age, gender, class and employment status group at each time point, and the second referring to the accuracy of the mortality rates applied to each group. This section takes a brief look at each and then explains how we can be confident that error in this work is at least minimal and random.

Among the first group of potential errors perhaps the most significant stems from the system used to allocate a social class to those not given one by the Census. The potential for error arises from the fact that the death rates applied to each social class group were derived from an analysis of the Longitudinal Study (LS) – an analysis which also involved giving a class to those without one, but which carried out that allocation in a different way. The LS is a data source based on *individuals*, and this provides a different basis for allocating a class. For example, a woman who looks after the home has no job in the formal

Figure 15: How class and unemployment explain the mortality map

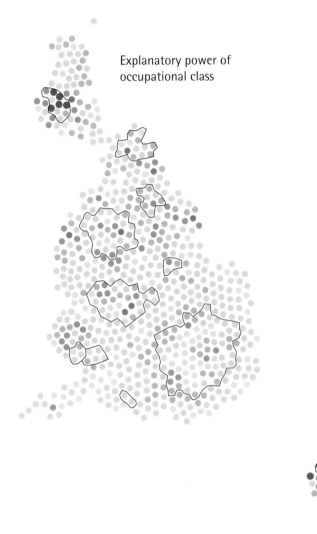

Explanatory power of
occupational class

Deaths explained (per 100 deaths)

- 0
- 1-4
- 5-7
- 8-10
- 11-13
- 14-41

Explanatory power of occupational
class and employment status
combined. Note the higher
explanatory power in the
North and West of Britain.

labour market and thus is not given a class by the Census. With LS data, there is other information about her as an individual which was used to allocate her to a class – the most obvious source being her partner's social class, if he has one (the Census processing system did not allow same-sex couples). Since the data employed in this report are held at an *area* level, there was no comparable information about individuals. Following the example given, the approach taken in this work was to allocate that woman to a class based on the class of her neighbours of the same age and gender who *did* work. It is important that the two models of class structure are as close as possible, since the LS is used to derive the rates of death for each age/gender/class group. Thus, if the LS system placed our example woman in class II and then she died, she would be contributing to the death rates for women of her age in class II. However, if the system used in this report had placed the woman in class IIIN, she would be in a different category of risk.

The method employed to minimise error from this source was to compare the age, gender, class group structure produced by our methods with that from the LS. If, for example, our methods had placed a higher proportion of men aged 60-64 in class IIIM than the LS model, adjustments could be made to reduce that proportion slightly and bring the two data sources into line. In fact we found that the two methods produced remarkably similar results for most age/gender groups. The greatest discrepancies were among the retired and women aged 50 or over. It was possible to adjust our technique to bring the models much closer together for these groups and the end result was a quite close match between the two data sets. Thus the potential for error was, at worst, minimised. The technical report describes this further.

A second component of error concerns the actual numbers of people, of each age, gender, class and employment status in Britain. Although the Census is often portrayed as the definitive count of people in Britain, the government accepts that it 'missed' over 1 million people in 1991 and that more people may be have been missed in some areas than others. Those most likely to have been missed are also, unfortunately, those with a relatively high risk of death. The missing people present a problem, because nearly everyone has their death recorded. So if a high number of deaths were found in an area in which fewer were

expected, it would not be possible to determine whether this is really an area with abnormally high rates of death, or if it is just that more people live there than the Census suggests and hence there are more deaths than expected. Estimates are available which correct basic age/gender counts to include the 'missing million' and these have been used where possible.

Another related source of potential error is that although the basic age/gender counts are as correct as possible, these data were further manipulated to yield an estimate of the number of people with each possible combination of age, gender, social class and employment status. It is the areas with the more extreme social structures that will have the greatest degree of error. To tackle this, the computer programmes used to estimate these vital counts contained an error-seeking function which alerted the operator when an 'extreme' area appeared to have been found. The age/gender/class counts were first estimated at ward level (an area of approximately 5,000 people) and, in such small areas, something like a large army barracks is sufficient to distort the age/gender/class profile of the population. In these 'extreme' cases, some potential error had to be accepted since there was no other way of proceeding with the method. Comfort can be drawn from the fact that just 11 (of over 10,000) wards fell into this category.

More error might stem from the national average death rates used to calculate the expected numbers of deaths in each constituency. Death rates by age, gender and class were available from the LS, but had to be derived for groups defined by their age, gender, class and employment status. It is important to recognise that the LS is a sample of only 1% of the population, that it is not a perfect sample and that it excludes Scotland. Fortunately a table of death rates by age, gender and class for both time periods was available. The ONS published variation in these rates by gender and class for both time periods was expanded to include a variation by employment status (Morris et al, 1994; Bunting, 1997).

So, it is clear that there were a number of potential sources of error in the methods used. There was, however, a useful means of detecting and correcting any systematic error in the results. If the model is working well, the national total number of expected deaths for an age/gender group (that is, for all constituencies summed together) ought to match the actual national total number of deaths in that group. The predicted total could be compared to the actual total and any systematic error would be seen as a difference between the two figures. If differences occurred in a regular pattern (for example, consistently higher numbers of deaths predicted for young men than actually took place) it would be a good indication that the models were incorrect. Some error was found, but it was very small and random in nature suggesting that the models were as good as they could be given the constraints which exist. It was also possible to use this information on error to improve the models slightly (to constrain them to account for the national total perfectly). In summary then, the constraints of available data and the techniques employed mean that the models are not perfect. However, in every instance possible the amount of error has been addressed and is believed to be minimal. The assumptions that have been made are also in all cases conservative. That is, their effect would be to reduce the efficiency of the model in accounting for inequalities in health across Britain.

Summary

This chapter has explained how the results shown in this report were constructed. The chapter has provided some of the details of how the calculations were made and what assumptions had to be adopted. A worked example for men in Sedgefield was given. Lastly, sources of possible error in this model were discussed.

- The key to this report is the relationship between the actual number of deaths which occurred in a parliamentary constituency and the number which were expected to occur.
- Most of the work undertaken for this report involved the manipulation of data which are publicly available into a format which would allow the calculations.
- There are potential sources of error in the work.
- We are confident that any errors are at least minimal and random.

7

Conclusion

This report looks in two directions – back in time to observe and explain changes in the geography of mortality which have occurred in Britain, and into a possible future where social policy has been effective in reducing those inequalities.

The geographical inequalities in Britain's health, as seen through premature mortality, rose between the early 1980s and the early 1990s to the highest levels yet recorded. This rise was steady and consistent (see Appendix B for figures). As ever, the North of Britain and its worse-off inner city areas experienced higher and higher rates of premature death in relative and sometimes absolute terms, while the South East and more affluent rural areas enjoyed lower and lower rates of premature death. This is perhaps no surprise but it is important to be able to connect the social policies of the time with their implications for health in an accounting framework which, in summary, illustrates that it was divisive social policies which accounted for rising inequalities in health.

A very significant finding is that it is possible to account for nearly all the geographical extent and change in premature mortality by understanding how the age, gender, social class and employment characteristics of Britain's population have changed and particularly how their distribution across the country has changed. An area's age/gender structure is becoming *less* important, while the socioeconomic status of its population becomes *more* important in explaining the deaths which occur there over time.

There has been no change in the power of social class to determine the geography of mortality – it remains a substantial contributor to an individual's socioeconomic position and hence to Britain's

unequal geography of death. Employment status, however, has become a much more important component of socioeconomic position and the geography of employment now accounts for a great deal more of the geography of mortality than it did 20 years ago.

If changes in the importance of socioeconomic position are responsible for growing inequalities in mortality, it is the meaning and distribution of socioeconomic position which must be tackled if these inequalities in health are to be dealt with effectively. The report shows the extent to which inequalities in health could be reduced if each of three current government targets are achieved – the attainment of full employment, a mild redistribution of income and the eradication of child poverty.

Modelling the potential effects of a successful implementation of these policies shows that, in every case, geographical inequalities in mortality are substantially reduced and a large number of premature deaths are avoided. In terms of numbers of lives saved, a mild redistribution of income would be the most valuable policy to implement. In terms of the proportion of lives saved, eradication of child poverty would have the biggest impact.

References

Bethune, A. (1997) 'Unemployment and mortality', in F. Drever and M. Whitehead (eds) *Health inequalities: Decennial supplement*, ONS Series DS No 15, London: The Stationery Office.

Blaxter, M. (1991) 'Fifty years on – inequalities in health', in M. Murphy and J. Hobcraft (eds) *Population research in Britain: A supplement to* Population Studies*, vol 45*, Cambridge: Cambridge University Press.

Bunting, J. (1997) 'Appendix A: Sources and methods', in F. Drever and M. Whitehead (eds) *Health inequalities: Decennial supplement*, ONS Series DS No 15, London: The Stationery Office.

Dobson, F. (1997) 'Government takes action to reduce health inequalities', DoH Press Release 97/192, in response to the Joseph Rowntree Publication *Death in Britain*, 11 August.

Dorling, D. (1995) *A new social atlas of Britain*, Chichester: John Wiley.

Dorling, D. (1997) *Death in Britain: How mortality rates have changed: 1950s-1990s*, York: Joseph Rowntree Foundation.

Drever, F. (1997) 'Appendix B', in F. Drever and M. Whitehead (eds) *Health inequalities: Decennial supplement*, ONS Series DS No 15, London: The Stationery Office.

Hattersley, L. (1999) 'Trends in life expectancy by social class – an update', *Health Statistics Quarterly*, vol 2, pp 16-24.

Martikainen, P. and Valkonen, T. (1996) 'Excess mortality of unemployed men and women during a period of rapidly increasing unemployment', *The Lancet*, no 348, pp 909-12.

Morris, J.K., Cook, D.G. and Shaper, A.G. (1994) 'Loss of employment and mortality', *British Medical Journal*, no 308, pp 1135-9.

Shaw, M., Gordon, D., Dorling, D. and Davey Smith, G. (1999) *The widening gap: Health inequalities and policy in Britain*, Bristol: The Policy Press.

Shaw, M., Orford S., Brimblecombe, N. and Dorling, D. (2000) 'Widening inequality in mortality between 160 regions of 15 countries of the European Union', *Social Science and Medicine*, vol 50, pp 1047-58.

Thompson, E.J. (ed) (1975) *Social Trends No 6*, London: HMSO.

Figure 16: Constituency map

Use this map and the key to find your own constituency. The areas labelled should help you find your way around the map. Constituency names are given in Appendix A.

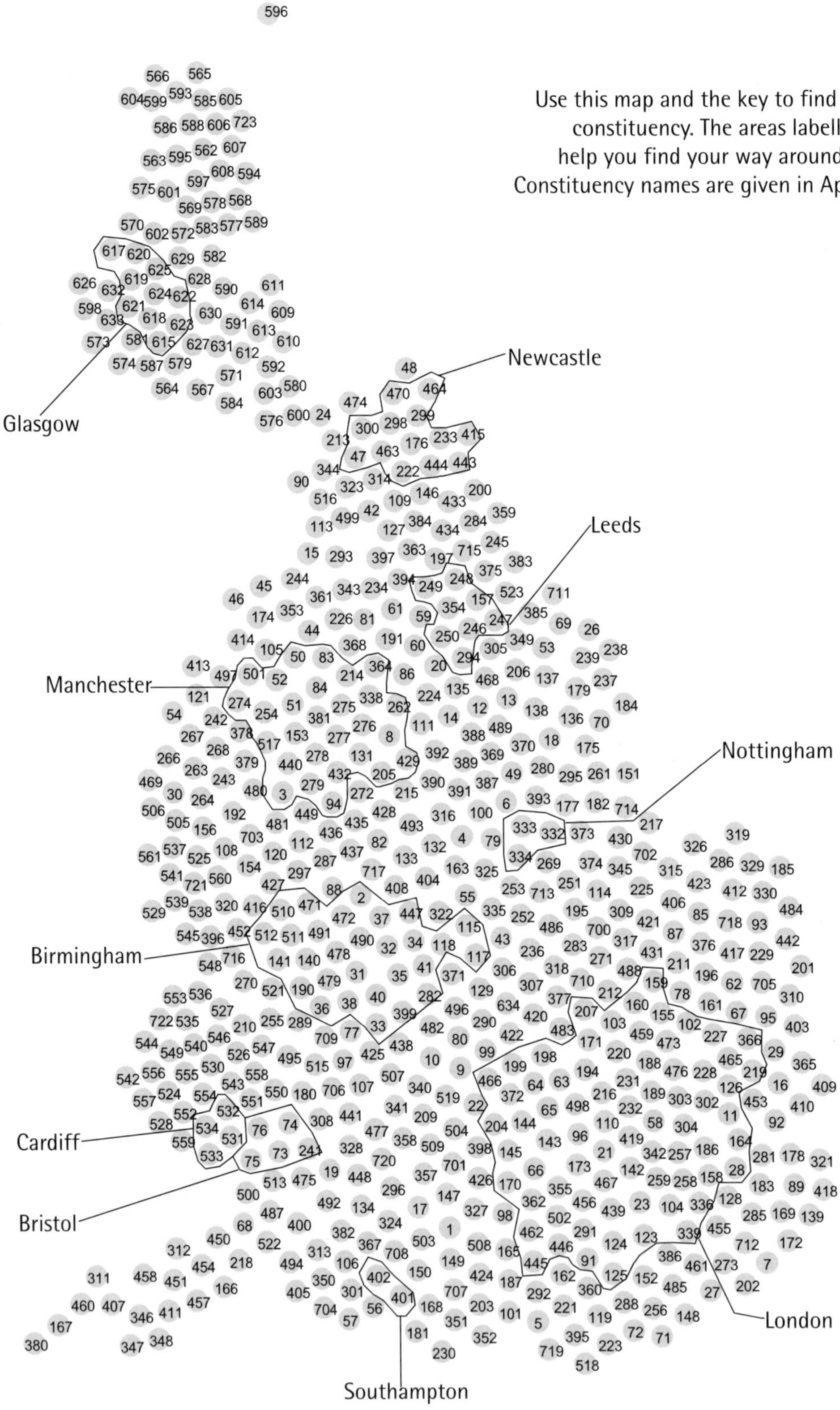

Appendix A: List of results by constituency

Constituencies are listed by 1991 county (region in Scotland). Figures are 1993 SMR (ages <65), lives saved per year by the attainment of full employment (ages 16-64), lives saved per year by a mild redistribution of wealth (ages 0-64), lives saved per year by eradication of child poverty (ages 0-14), total lives saved (0-65).

ID		SMR	Full	Redis	Erad	Total
Avon						
19	Bath	85	2	13	2	17
73	Bristol East	105	4	15	3	22
74	Bristol North West	99	3	15	3	21
75	Bristol South	104	5	16	3	24
76	Bristol West	100	3	9	1	14
241	Kingswood	84	3	14	2	20
308	Northavon	74	2	14	2	18
475	Wansdyke	77	2	12	1	15
500	Weston super Mare	93	3	13	2	17
513	Woodspring	67	2	12	1	15
Bedfordshire						
271	Luton South	115	4	12	4	20
283	Mid Bedfordshire	79	2	10	1	14
309	Bedford	97	3	12	2	17
318	Luton North	99	4	13	3	19
420	South West Bedfordshire	87	2	12	2	17
700	North East Bedfordshire	91	2	11	1	14
Berkshire						
147	Bracknell	81	2	11	2	15
296	Newbury	86	1	11	2	15
324	North West Hampshire	77	2	13	2	17
357	Reading East	87	2	12	2	17
358	Reading West	93	2	13	2	18
398	Slough	111	3	13	4	19
504	Maidenhead	81	1	11	1	13
509	Wokingham	69	1	9	1	11
701	Windsor	78	1	10	1	13

ID		SMR	Full	Redis	Erad	Total
Borders						
600	Roxburgh and Berwickshire	101	2	9	1	12
603	Tweeddale Ettrick and Lauderdale	92	2	7	1	10
Buckinghamshire						
9	Aylesbury	85	2	13	2	18
22	Beaconsfield	74	1	10	1	13
80	Buckingham	75	1	9	1	12
99	Chesham and Amersham	70	1	10	1	12
290	Milton Keynes South West	107	3	12	3	18
422	South West Hertfordshire	79	2	10	2	13
519	Wycombe	87	2	12	2	16
634	Milton Keynes North East	82	2	8	2	12
Cambridgeshire						
87	Cambridge	82	2	12	2	16
225	Huntingdon	82	2	14	2	19
315	North East Cambridgeshire	99	3	16	3	22
345	Peterborough	99	5	13	4	22
406	South East Cambridgeshire	77	2	13	2	16
421	South Cambridgeshire	70	1	11	1	14
423	South West Norfolk	87	4	18	3	25
702	North West Cambridgeshire	85	3	12	2	18

ID		SMR	Full	Redis	Erad	Total
Central						
569	Ochil	119	5	10	1	16
582	Falkirk East	107	7	12	1	20
583	Falkirk West	126	6	9	1	17
601	Stirling	122	3	8	1	12
Cheshire						
108	City of Chester	99	4	10	2	16
112	Congleton	89	3	11	2	16
120	Crewe and Nantwich	98	3	13	3	20
154	Eddisbury	97	3	11	2	16
156	Ellesmere Port and Neston	104	6	12	3	21
192	Halton	117	5	14	3	22
272	Macclesfield	87	3	11	2	15
449	Tatton	89	2	9	1	11
480	Warrington North	118	5	12	3	20
481	Warrington South	103	4	11	2	17
703	Weaver Vale	101	4	11	3	18
Cleveland						
200	Hartlepool	126	8	15	4	27
245	Middlesbrough South and East Cleveland	114	6	13	3	22
284	Middlesbrough	145	10	17	5	32
359	Redcar	120	7	16	3	26
433	Stockton North	128	7	14	4	25
434	Stockton South	105	5	10	2	18
Clwyd						
525	Alyn and Deeside	105	3	12	2	17
537	Clwyd West	95	2	9	2	13
538	Clwyd South	103	3	11	2	16
541	Delyn	107	3	11	2	17
560	Wrexham	108	3	10	2	15
721	Vale of Clwyd	110	3	9	2	14
Cornwall						
167	Falmouth and Camborne	100	5	15	2	22
311	North Cornwall	87	4	17	2	23
380	St Ives	93	4	15	2	22
407	South East Cornwall	82	4	16	2	21
460	Truro and St Austell	92	4	16	2	22
Cumbria						
15	Barrow and Furness	114	3	14	2	19
90	Carlisle	116	3	12	2	17
113	Copeland	112	3	13	3	18
344	Penrith and the Border	91	2	11	2	15
499	Westmorland and Lonsdale	84	1	12	1	15
516	Workington	107	5	14	3	22

ID		SMR	Full	Redis	Erad	Total
Derbyshire						
4	Amber Valley	104	4	16	2	22
49	Bolsover	108	4	15	2	21
100	Chesterfield	110	4	13	2	20
132	Derby North	104	4	13	2	20
133	Derby South	113	6	13	4	23
163	Erewash	98	4	15	2	22
215	High Peak	96	3	13	2	18
316	North East Derbyshire	92	5	14	2	21
404	South Derbyshire	94	3	15	2	19
493	West Derbyshire	82	2	14	1	17
Devon						
166	Exeter	98	3	15	2	20
218	East Devon	75	2	12	2	16
312	North Devon	89	2	14	2	19
346	Plymouth Devonport	110	5	20	4	29
347	Plymouth Sutton	115	5	14	3	22
348	South West Devon	79	2	11	2	15
411	Totnes	77	3	13	2	18
451	Teignbridge	87	3	15	2	20
454	Tiverton and Honiton	81	2	14	2	18
457	Torbay	97	4	13	2	19
458	Torridge and West Devon	90	3	16	2	20
Dorset						
56	Bournemouth East	102	3	10	1	14
57	Bournemouth West	94	3	10	2	15
106	Christchurch	73	2	11	1	14
313	North Dorset	76	2	11	2	15
350	Poole	95	2	10	2	14
405	South Dorset	93	2	12	2	17
494	West Dorset	85	2	12	2	16
704	Mid Dorset and North Poole	77	2	14	2	18
Dumfries and Galloway						
576	Dumfries	107	4	12	2	17
584	Galloway and Upper Nithsdale	117	4	10	1	15
Durham						
42	Bishop Auckland	113	6	15	3	23
109	City of Durham	97	4	13	2	20
127	Darlington	119	6	12	3	21
146	Easington	133	5	14	3	23
314	North Durham	102	6	13	3	22
323	North West Durham	118	6	13	2	22
384	Sedgefield	118	5	13	2	20

ID		SMR	Full	Redis	Erad	Total
Dyfed						
535	Carmarthen East and Dinefwr	107	3	11	2	15
536	Ceredigion	97	2	9	1	13
544	Llanelli	106	4	12	2	18
553	Preseli Pembrokeshire	102	3	10	2	16
722	Carmarthen West and South Pembrokeshire	95	3	10	2	15
East Sussex						
27	Bexhill and Battle	77	2	9	1	12
71	Brighton Kemptown	116	3	12	2	17
72	Brighton Pavilion	108	3	9	1	13
148	Eastbourne	90	2	10	2	14
202	Hastings and Rye	104	3	12	2	18
223	Hove	103	3	9	1	13
256	Lewes	85	2	10	1	12
485	Wealden	80	1	12	2	15
Essex						
16	Basildon	92	4	15	3	22
29	Billericay	86	3	11	2	16
62	Braintree	79	2	12	2	17
67	Brentwood and Ongar	79	2	10	1	13
92	Castle Point	82	2	13	1	16
95	West Chelmsford	72	2	11	2	15
161	Epping Forest	85	2	11	1	15
196	Harlow	90	3	12	2	17
201	Harwich	96	4	12	2	18
310	Colchester	93	2	12	3	17
365	Rayleigh	78	2	10	1	13
376	Saffron Walden	74	2	12	2	16
403	Maldon and East Chelmsford	86	2	12	1	15
409	Rochford and Southend East	105	3	11	2	16
410	Southend West	79	2	9	1	12
453	Thurrock	107	5	13	4	21
705	North Essex	80	2	12	1	16
Fife						
568	Central Fife	121	5	12	2	18
577	Dunfermline East	119	4	11	2	17
578	Dunfermline West	124	3	6	1	11
589	Kirkcaldy	117	5	10	1	16
594	North East Fife	96	2	7	1	10
Gloucestershire						
97	Cheltenham	95	3	11	2	16
107	Cotswold	77	2	12	2	16
180	Gloucester	102	3	14	4	22

ID		SMR	Full	Redis	Erad	Total
Gloucestershire cont						
441	Stroud	78	2	15	2	19
495	Forest .of Dean	94	3	13	2	18
706	Tewkesbury	80	2	12	2	15
Grampian						
565	Banff and Buchan	106	4	12	2	18
585	Gordon	97	2	9	1	12
588	West Aberdeenshire and Kincardine	85	1	6	1	9
593	Moray	106	3	11	2	16
605	Aberdeen North	116	2	8	1	11
606	Aberdeen South	99	2	8	1	11
723	Aberdeen Central	128	3	10	1	14
Greater London						
143	Acton and Shepherds Bush	132	5	13	2	21
11	Barking	118	3	10	3	16
21	Battersea	124	4	11	2	17
23	Beckenham	87	2	8	1	12
28	Bexleyheath and Crayford	84	2	10	1	13
58	Bethnal Green and Bow	138	9	15	6	29
63	Brent East	120	4	11	2	16
64	Brent North	88	2	8	1	11
65	Brent South	120	4	14	3	21
66	Brentford and Isleworth	104	3	11	2	16
104	Bromley and Chislehurst	83	2	10	1	13
342	Camberwell and Peckham	141	6	10	4	20
91	Carshalton and Wallington	93	2	11	2	15
102	Chingford and Woodford Green	81	2	8	1	11
103	Chipping Barnet	77	2	8	1	11
110	Cities of London and Westminster	98	6	15	1	23
123	Croydon Central	94	3	12	2	17
124	Croydon North	106	3	13	3	19
125	Croydon South	77	2	9	1	12
126	Dagenham	106	3	11	3	17
257	Deptford	128	5	9	3	16
142	Dulwich and West Norwood	121	5	10	2	17
144	Ealing North	93	3	12	2	18
302	East Ham	122	5	11	5	21
155	Edmonton	98	3	10	2	16
158	Eltham	93	3	9	2	14
159	Enfield North	91	3	12	2	17

51

ID		SMR	Full	Redis	Erad	Total
Greater London cont						
164	Erith and Thamesmead	105	4	10	3	17
170	Feltham and Heston	105	3	14	3	20
171	Finchley and Golders Green	83	3	10	1	13
173	Hammersmith and Fulham	140	5	14	2	20
186	Greenwich and Woolwich	124	4	10	4	18
188	Hackney North and Stoke Newington	137	7	9	3	19
189	Hackney South and Shoreditch	141	7	13	4	24
194	Hampstead and Highgate	111	4	10	1	15
198	Harrow East	89	2	12	2	16
199	Harrow West	79	2	10	1	13
204	Hayes and Harlington	108	2	10	2	15
207	Hendon	87	3	11	2	15
216	Holborn and St Pancras	155	5	12	2	19
219	Hornchurch	92	2	11	1	14
220	Hornsey and Wood Green	102	4	11	2	17
227	Ilford North	91	2	9	2	13
228	Ilford South	99	3	9	2	14
231	Islington North	132	6	11	3	19
232	Islington South and Finsbury	130	5	11	2	19
96	Kensington and Chelsea	102	4	12	1	17
445	Kingston and Surbiton	84	2	11	1	14
258	Lewisham East	112	3	8	2	13
259	Lewisham West	106	3	8	2	13
476	Leyton and Wanstead	108	3	9	3	15
291	Mitcham and Morden	101	3	10	2	16
336	Old Bexley and Sidcup	76	2	11	1	14
339	Orpington	80	2	12	2	16
304	Poplar and Canning Town	147	8	14	5	28
355	Putney	110	3	9	1	13
498	Regents Park and Kensington North	135	7	17	3	27
362	Richmond Park	84	2	9	1	12
366	Romford	84	2	10	1	13
372	Ruislip-Northwood	84	1	8	1	10
160	Southgate	78	2	9	1	12
145	Southall	117	5	14	3	22

ID		SMR	Full	Redis	Erad	Total
Greater London cont						
419	Southwark North and Bermondsey	156	6	12	4	22
439	Streatham	126	5	11	2	18
446	Sutton and Cheam	86	1	8	1	11
456	Tooting	118	3	10	1	15
459	Tottenham	126	6	16	4	26
462	Twickenham	81	2	9	1	12
465	Upminster	88	2	9	1	13
466	Uxbridge	88	2	10	2	13
467	Vauxhall	157	7	15	4	26
473	Walthamstow	114	3	9	3	15
303	West Ham	131	5	11	4	20
502	Wimbledon	81	2	7	1	10
Greater Manchester						
3	Altrincham and Sale West	91	3	8	1	12
8	Ashton under Lyne	131	6	15	3	24
50	Bolton North East	123	6	13	3	22
51	Bolton South East	139	6	13	4	23
52	Bolton West	95	3	10	2	14
83	Bury North	101	3	12	2	17
84	Bury South	107	3	10	2	15
94	Cheadle	73	2	8	1	11
131	Denton and Reddish	112	5	12	2	20
153	Eccles	128	7	13	3	23
205	Hazel Grove	93	3	10	1	14
214	Heywood and Middleton	119	7	13	3	23
254	Leigh	118	5	16	3	24
262	Oldham East and Saddleworth	125	5	13	3	21
274	Makerfield	114	6	14	3	23
275	Manchester Blackley	171	8	13	5	26
276	Manchester Central	176	11	16	5	33
277	Manchester Gorton	158	5	9	3	17
278	Manchester Withington	127	4	9	2	15
338	Oldham West and Royton	124	6	14	4	24
364	Rochdale	133	6	12	4	22
381	Salford	164	8	12	3	24
429	Stalybridge and Hyde	117	5	12	3	20
432	Stockport	118	4	9	3	16
440	Stretford and Urmston	108	6	12	3	20
501	Wigan	107	6	14	3	22
279	Wythenshawe and Sale East	130	6	12	4	22
517	Worsley	116	5	12	3	20

ID		SMR	Full	Redis	Erad	Total
Gwent						
526	Blaenau Gwent	117	5	14	3	22
543	Islwyn	104	3	11	2	17
547	Monmouth	82	2	11	2	15
550	Newport East	109	4	11	3	18
551	Newport West	107	4	10	2	16
558	Torfaen	115	4	12	3	19
Gwynedd						
529	Caernarfon	99	3	8	2	13
539	Conwy	97	3	10	2	15
545	Merionnydd nant Conwy	95	2	6	1	9
561	Ynys Mon	107	4	11	2	16
Hampshire						
1	Aldershot	90	2	13	2	17
17	Basingstoke	88	2	13	2	18
149	East Hampshire	84	2	13	2	17
150	Eastleigh	86	2	10	2	14
168	Fareham	80	2	12	1	16
181	Gosport	91	2	11	2	16
203	Havant	97	3	14	2	19
367	New Forest East	83	2	12	2	16
301	New Forest West	78	2	9	1	13
707	North East Hampshire	75	1	11	1	13
351	Portsmouth North	100	3	11	2	16
352	Portsmouth South	114	4	16	3	23
708	Romsey	68	2	11	1	14
401	Southampton Itchen	111	5	15	3	22
402	Southampton Test	113	4	13	3	19
503	Winchester	77	2	13	2	16
Hereford and Worcester						
77	Bromsgrove	83	3	12	2	17
210	Hereford	87	3	12	3	17
255	Leominster	80	2	12	2	15
709	Mid Worcestershire	87	2	12	2	16
289	Redditch	87	3	10	2	16
425	West Worcestershire	77	2	11	1	15
515	Worcester	100	3	11	2	16
521	Wyre Forest	96	4	16	2	22
Hertfordshire						
78	Broxbourne	83	2	12	2	15
496	Hemel Hempstead	79	2	11	2	15
211	Hertford and Stortford	79	2	11	1	14
212	Hertsmere	83	2	9	1	12
710	Hitchin and Harpenden	80	2	9	1	12

ID		SMR	Full	Redis	Erad	Total
Hertfordshire cont						
317	North East Hertfordshire	80	2	12	2	16
377	St Albans	81	1	10	1	13
431	Stevenage	83	3	10	2	14
483	Watford	86	2	11	2	15
488	Welwyn Hatfield	85	2	10	2	13
Highland						
566	Caithness Sutherland and Easter Ross	120	3	8	1	12
586	Inverness East Nairn and Lochaber	106	3	11	2	15
599	Ross Skye and Inverness West	116	4	10	2	15
Humberside						
26	Haltemprice and Howden	78	2	10	1	14
53	Brigg and Goole	106	5	14	2	21
69	Beverley and Holderness	83	3	12	2	17
70	Cleethorpes	103	5	14	3	22
711	East Yorkshire	95	3	13	2	19
184	Great Grimsby	124	7	15	5	26
237	Hull East	124	8	17	6	31
238	Hull North	108	5	11	3	20
239	Hull West and Hessle	120	7	15	3	25
179	Scunthorpe	113	6	15	3	24
Islands						
596	Orkney and Shetland	103	2	6	1	9
604	Western Isles	125	3	4	1	8
Isle of Wight						
230	Isle of Wight	91	5	19	3	27
Kent						
7	Ashford	87	3	13	2	18
89	Canterbury	85	3	14	2	18
285	Chatham and Aylesford	99	3	12	3	17
128	Dartford	93	2	12	2	16
139	Dover	103	3	12	3	18
712	Faversham and Mid Kent	81	2	12	2	16
172	Folkestone and Hythe	93	3	13	2	19
178	Gillingham	88	3	12	3	18
183	Gravesham	90	4	13	3	19
273	Maidstone and the Weald	84	2	13	2	16
281	Medway	102	3	12	2	17

ID		SMR	Full	Redis	Erad	Total
Kent cont						
321	North Thanet	106	3	11	2	17
386	Sevenoaks	81	2	10	1	13
169	Sittingbourne and Sheppey	99	3	14	2	19
418	South Thanet	97	4	11	2	17
455	Tonbridge and Malling	74	2	11	1	14
461	Tunbridge Wells	79	2	10	2	13
Lancashire						
44	Blackburn	132	6	14	5	25
45	Blackpool North and Fleetwood	116	5	13	2	20
46	Blackpool South	135	6	16	3	25
81	Burnley	128	5	12	3	21
105	Chorley	94	3	12	2	18
174	Fylde	95	2	10	2	14
226	Hyndburn	117	4	13	3	19
244	Lancaster and Wyre	95	3	11	2	16
293	Morecambe and Lunesdale	105	4	11	2	17
343	Pendle	110	4	12	3	18
353	Preston	139	7	16	4	28
361	Ribble Valley	101	2	11	1	14
368	Rossendale and Darwen	113	4	12	2	17
414	South Ribble	96	3	11	2	16
497	West Lancashire	98	6	13	3	22
Leicestershire						
43	Blaby	79	2	11	1	14
55	Bosworth	87	2	13	1	16
713	Charnwood	79	2	13	1	16
195	Harborough	80	2	11	1	14
251	Leicester East	115	5	12	3	20
252	Leicester South	112	5	12	3	21
253	Leicester West	123	6	13	3	22
269	Loughborough	84	2	11	1	15
325	North West Leicestershire	90	2	13	2	17
374	Rutland and Melton	82	2	13	2	17
Lincolnshire						
217	Boston and Skegness	103	4	14	2	20
175	Gainsborough	94	3	13	2	18
714	Grantham and Stamford	94	3	13	2	18
261	Lincoln	117	5	12	2	19
151	Louth and Horncastle	101	4	14	2	19
182	Sleaford and North Hykeham	87	2	14	2	18

ID		SMR	Full	Redis	Erad	Total
Lincolnshire cont						
430	South Holland and the Deepings	96	2	14	2	18
Lothian						
580	East Lothian	101	3	8	1	13
609	Edinburgh Central	138	4	8	1	12
610	Edinburgh East and Musselburgh	125	5	8	2	14
611	Edinburgh North and Leith	145	7	10	2	19
612	Edinburgh Pentlands	99	3	6	1	10
613	Edinburgh South	109	3	6	1	10
614	Edinburgh West	96	2	7	1	10
590	Linlithgow	121	7	11	1	20
591	Livingston	122	5	9	2	16
592	Midlothian	122	4	9	1	14
Merseyside						
30	Birkenhead	149	8	12	4	24
54	Bootle	140	10	12	4	26
121	Crosby	99	4	7	1	12
242	Knowsley North and Sefton East	115	11	14	3	28
243	Knowsley South	121	10	14	4	28
263	Liverpool Wavertree	123	9	11	3	23
264	Liverpool Garston	120	9	12	3	24
266	Liverpool Riverside	174	14	15	4	34
267	Liverpool Walton	139	11	14	4	30
268	Liverpool West Derby	138	11	14	4	29
378	St Helens North	109	6	14	2	22
379	St Helens South	121	7	15	3	24
413	Southport	103	3	9	1	13
469	Wallasey	127	6	11	3	21
505	Wirral South	88	4	9	1	14
506	Wirral West	88	4	8	1	13
Mid Glamorgan						
528	Bridgend	99	3	10	2	15
530	Caerphilly	108	4	14	3	21
540	Cynon Valley	123	4	11	2	17
546	Merthyr Tydfil and Rhymney	124	5	13	3	21
552	Ogmore	116	4	12	3	19
554	Pontypridd	104	4	13	2	19
555	Rhondda	127	5	13	3	21

ID		SMR	Full	Redis	Erad	Total
Norfolk						
185	Great Yarmouth	101	5	14	2	21
286	Mid Norfolk	78	3	14	2	18
319	North Norfolk	84	3	15	2	20
326	North West Norfolk	91	5	16	3	23
329	Norwich North	85	3	15	2	21
330	Norwich South	95	4	13	2	19
412	South Norfolk	70	3	14	2	19
North Yorkshire						
523	City of York	102	3	15	3	22
197	Harrogate and Knaresborough	93	2	9	2	13
363	Richmond	84	2	12	2	16
375	Ryedale	81	2	12	2	16
383	Scarborough and Whitby	96	4	14	3	21
385	Selby	88	3	13	2	17
397	Skipton and Ripon	86	1	12	2	15
715	Vale of York	83	2	11	2	15
Northamptonshire						
114	Corby	115	5	14	2	21
129	Daventry	80	2	13	2	17
236	Kettering	89	3	13	2	18
306	Northampton North	102	3	13	3	19
307	Northampton South	101	3	12	2	17
486	Wellingborough	90	3	14	2	19
Northumberland						
24	Berwick upon Tweed	95	3	11	2	16
48	Blyth Valley	107	4	12	2	18
213	Hexham	87	2	10	1	13
474	Wansbeck	112	4	13	3	19
Nottinghamshire						
6	Ashfield	102	4	17	2	24
18	Bassetlaw	104	4	16	2	22
79	Broxtowe	83	3	12	2	17
177	Gedling	91	3	12	1	16
280	Mansfield	104	4	14	2	20
295	Newark	102	3	14	2	19
332	Nottingham East	138	7	14	3	24
333	Nottingham North	126	5	14	4	24
334	Nottingham South	112	5	13	2	21
373	Rushcliffe	82	2	11	1	14
393	Sherwood	97	4	15	2	21
Oxfordshire						
10	Banbury	83	2	13	3	19
209	Henley	75	2	11	2	14
340	Oxford East	103	3	14	3	20

ID		SMR	Full	Redis	Erad	Total
Oxfordshire cont						
341	Oxford West and Abingdon	78	2	12	1	16
477	Wantage	76	2	12	2	16
507	Witney	72	2	12	2	16
Powys						
527	Brecon and Radnorshire	96	2	10	2	13
548	Montgomeryshire	93	2	8	1	11
Shropshire						
270	Ludlow	81	3	11	2	16
320	North Shropshire	92	3	13	2	18
396	Shrewsbury and Atcham	90	2	12	2	17
452	Telford	102	5	12	3	20
716	The Wrekin	100	3	11	2	17
Somerset						
68	Bridgwater	85	3	15	3	21
400	Somerton and Frome	79	2	14	2	19
450	Taunton	89	3	14	2	19
487	Wells	91	2	13	2	17
522	Yeovil	82	2	14	2	19
South Glamorgan						
531	Cardiff Central	98	3	10	2	15
532	Cardiff North	90	2	5	1	8
533	Cardiff South and Penarth	119	5	11	3	19
534	Cardiff West	117	4	9	3	16
559	Vale of Glamorgan	94	3	11	2	17
South Yorkshire						
12	Barnsley Central	121	6	14	3	23
13	Barnsley East and Mexborough	113	6	15	4	25
14	Barnsley West and Penistone	105	5	13	3	20
136	Doncaster Central	106	6	13	3	22
137	Doncaster North	118	6	14	3	24
138	Don Valley	100	5	13	3	21
369	Rotherham	114	6	12	3	22
370	Rother Valley	104	5	14	3	22
387	Sheffield Attercliffe	103	6	14	3	22
388	Sheffield Brightside	127	7	15	4	26
389	Sheffield Central	127	9	14	4	27
390	Sheffield Hallam	68	2	6	1	8
391	Sheffield Heeley	104	7	14	3	24
392	Sheffield Hillsborough	95	5	15	2	22
489	Wentworth	109	6	15	3	23

ID		SMR	Full	Redis	Erad	Total	ID		SMR	Full	Redis	Erad	Total
Staffordshire							**Strathclyde cont**						
82	Burton	99	4	14	3	21	587	Kilmarnock and Loudoun	123	6	12	2	20
88	Cannock Chase	106	4	15	2	21	631	Motherwell and Wishaw	145	7	10	1	18
717	Lichfield	87	3	12	2	16							
297	Newcastle under Lyme	105	3	13	2	19	632	Paisley North	144	7	11	1	19
408	Tamworth	100	4	13	2	19	633	Paisley South	138	7	11	1	20
416	South Staffordshire	78	3	12	1	16	602	Strathkelvin and Bearsden	101	4	7	1	12
427	Stafford	90	3	11	2	16							
428	Staffordshire Moorlands	99	3	15	2	19	598	West Renfrewshire	124	5	7	1	12
435	Stoke Central	137	4	15	3	22	**Suffolk**						
436	Stoke North	123	4	14	2	20	718	Bury St Edmunds	76	2	14	2	19
437	Stoke South	113	4	15	3	21	93	Central Suffolk and North Ipswich	78	2	14	2	18
287	Stone	99	2	12	1	16							
Strathclyde							229	Ipswich	96	3	12	2	18
628	Airdrie and Shotts	152	7	12	2	21	417	South Suffolk	71	2	12	1	16
563	Argyll and Bute	128	4	9	1	14	442	Suffolk Coastal	72	2	13	2	18
564	Ayr	117	4	7	1	12	484	Waveney	99	4	15	2	21
567	Carrick Cumnock and Doon Valley	119	8	15	2	24	85	West Suffolk	83	2	14	3	20
570	Clydebank and Milngavie	126	5	8	1	15	**Surrey**						
							152	East Surrey	81	2	11	1	14
571	Clydesdale	117	5	11	1	17	162	Epsom and Ewell	82	1	9	1	12
629	Coatbridge and Chryston	145	7	11	1	19	165	Esher and Walton	72	1	9	1	12
							187	Guildford	77	1	11	2	14
572	Cumbernauld and Kilsyth	125	4	8	1	13	292	Mole Valley	74	1	10	1	13
							360	Reigate	89	1	8	1	11
573	Cunninghame North	128	6	9	1	16	98	Runnymede and Weybridge	80	1	11	1	13
574	Cunninghame South	140	6	11	2	18							
575	Dumbarton	133	6	9	1	16	424	South West Surrey	76	1	11	1	13
579	East Kilbride	113	5	9	1	15	426	Spelthorne	79	2	11	2	14
581	Eastwood	88	4	5	1	9	327	Surrey Heath	77	2	11	1	14
617	Glasgow Anniesland	175	7	9	2	18	508	Woking	75	1	10	2	13
622	Glasgow Baillieston	180	10	12	2	24	**Tayside**						
615	Glasgow Cathcart	150	5	7	1	14	562	Angus	106	3	9	1	13
618	Glasgow Govan	172	8	7	2	17	607	Dundee East	134	9	12	2	23
619	Glasgow Kelvin	158	5	6	0	12	608	Dundee West	138	7	11	2	20
620	Glasgow Maryhill	197	12	13	2	27	595	North Tayside	97	3	11	1	15
621	Glasgow Pollock	181	11	12	2	24	597	Perth	120	3	9	1	14
623	Glasgow Rutherglen	153	8	8	1	17	**Tyne and Wear**						
							47	Blaydon	103	5	12	2	19
624	Glasgow Shettleston	228	11	11	2	23	176	Gateshead East and Washington West	114	7	15	3	24
625	Glasgow Springburn	213	12	13	2	27	222	Houghton and Washington East	130	5	11	2	18
626	Greenock and Inverclyde	163	8	10	1	19	233	Jarrow	125	7	12	2	21
							298	Newcastle Central	123	6	10	2	18
627	Hamilton South	146	5	10	1	16	299	Newcastle East and Wallsend	130	7	13	3	22
630	Hamilton North and Bellshill	153	8	12	2	21							
							300	Newcastle North	102	6	11	2	19
							470	North Tyneside	116	5	13	3	21

ID		SMR	Full	Redis	Erad	Total
Tyne and Wear cont						
415	South Shields	124	7	13	3	23
443	Sunderland North	122	9	14	3	25
444	Sunderland South	119	10	15	3	27
463	Tyne Bridge	159	10	15	4	29
464	Tynemouth	104	5	10	2	17
Warwickshire						
322	North Warwickshire	94	4	15	3	22
335	Nuneaton	98	4	14	3	21
371	Rugby and Kenilworth	92	3	13	2	18
438	Stratford on Avon	83	2	14	2	18
482	Warwick and Leamington	97	3	12	2	17
West Glamorgan						
524	Aberavon	113	4	12	3	19
542	Gower	93	3	10	2	14
549	Neath	116	4	11	2	17
556	Swansea East	118	5	12	3	20
557	Swansea West	106	5	11	2	17
West Midlands						
2	Aldridge-Brownhills	89	4	13	2	18
31	Birmingham Edgbaston	110	7	13	3	23
32	Birmingham Erdington	139	9	16	4	28
33	Birmingham Hall Green	105	5	11	2	18
34	Birmingham Hodge Hill	124	7	12	3	22
35	Birmingham Ladywood	151	14	17	8	39
36	Birmingham Northfield	109	4	8	2	14
37	Birmingham Perry Barr	110	6	14	4	24
38	Birmingham Selly Oak	115	4	9	2	15
40	Birmingham Sparkbrook and Small Heath	144	11	16	7	33
41	Birmingham Yardley	109	4	9	2	15
115	Coventry North East	119	8	15	5	27
117	Coventry South	114	6	12	3	20
118	Coventry North West	107	6	14	3	23
140	Dudley North	104	6	17	3	26
141	Dudley South	100	5	14	2	21
479	Halesowen and Rowley Regis	99	4	11	2	17
282	Meriden	93	5	14	3	22

ID		SMR	Full	Redis	Erad	Total
West Midlands cont						
399	Solihull	75	3	10	1	14
190	Stourbridge	88	4	12	2	18
447	Sutton Coldfield	76	3	8	1	12
471	Walsall North	126	6	16	3	25
472	Walsall South	119	6	13	3	22
478	Warley	122	6	12	3	22
490	West Bromwich East	118	7	15	3	24
491	West Bromwich West	124	7	15	3	26
510	Wolverhampton North East	115	6	13	3	22
511	Wolverhampton South East	125	8	14	3	25
512	Wolverhampton South West	103	5	10	2	17
West Sussex						
719	Arundel and South Downs	73	1	10	1	13
5	Bognor Regis and Littlehampton	100	2	11	2	15
101	Chichester	82	2	12	2	15
119	Crawley	90	2	12	3	17
221	Horsham	77	1	9	1	12
288	Mid Sussex	77	1	11	1	13
395	Worthing East and Shoreham	88	2	12	2	15
518	Worthing West	90	1	8	1	10
West Yorkshire						
20	Batley and Spen	108	5	14	3	22
59	Bradford North	127	7	14	5	25
60	Bradford South	119	5	13	4	22
61	Bradford West	135	9	14	6	29
86	Calder Valley	104	3	12	2	18
111	Colne Valley	97	5	14	3	22
135	Dewsbury	109	3	10	3	16
157	Elmet	91	3	12	2	16
191	Halifax	124	5	14	4	23
206	Hemsworth	109	5	16	3	25
224	Huddersfield	115	4	10	3	17
234	Keighley	97	4	11	3	17
246	Leeds Central	143	8	17	4	29
247	Leeds East	124	6	13	4	22
248	Leeds North East	91	4	7	2	13
249	Leeds North West	87	3	9	1	13
250	Leeds West	113	5	13	3	22
294	Morley and Rothwell	99	4	13	2	19
305	Normanton	106	3	10	2	15
349	Pontefract and Castleford	117	5	15	4	24

ID		SMR	Full	Redis	Erad	Total
West Yorkshire cont						
354	Pudsey	86	3	12	2	16
394	Shipley	97	3	10	2	14
468	Wakefield	104	4	14	2	20
Wiltshire						
134	Devizes	84	2	14	3	20
328	North Wiltshire	81	2	14	3	18
382	Salisbury	88	2	14	3	19
448	Swindon North	90	2	11	2	16
720	Swindon South	94	4	12	3	19
492	Westbury	83	2	14	2	18

Appendix B: Evidence of a still widening health gap

The precursor to this report, *Death in Britain* (Dorling, 1997) presented statistics which showed that, by 1992, inequalities in mortality had risen to their highest levels since at least the 1930s. The starting point for this report was to update those statistics to the end of 1998 (the latest data available), to determine whether the 'gap' is still widening. The geographical areas used for this historical comparison are not parliamentary constituencies. This is because historical data were not published for constituencies, making it impossible to follow changes accurately through time at that spatial scale. Instead, *Death in Britain* used old county borough boundaries and in order to update it, those boundaries have had to be used again. At each time period for which data are available, Britain is divided into 10 equal-sized groups of areas in terms of population – these are called deciles. The SMR of each of

these groups is then calculated (see Chapter 2 for a definition of SMR). SMRs which are greater than 100 indicate higher chances of mortality, and those less than 100 indicate lower chances of mortality, all relative to the national average. The results are shown below.

The table shows starkly that the inequalities in mortality reported in *Death in Britain* that were at their highest ever recorded level by 1992 continued to rise throughout the period 1993 to 1998. In 1992 all people living in the decile areas with the highest mortality rates were 42% more likely to die prematurely than the national average. This rose to a rate 50% higher than the national average in the latest time period. Relative mortality ratios also rose for the second, third and fourth deciles (the 2nd, 3rd and 4th highest mortality groups of areas) which illustrates

Standardised mortality ratios for deaths <65 in Britain by deciles of population (grouped by old county borough and ordered by SMR), Britain (1950–98)

Decile	1950–53	1959–63	1969–73	1981–85	1986–89	1990–92	1993–95	1996–98
1	131	136	131	135	139	142	147	150
2	118	123	116	119	121	121	121	122
3	112	117	112	114	114	111	113	114
4	107	111	108	110	107	105	107	108
5	103	105	103	102	102	99	99	99
6	99	97	97	96	96	94	95	96
7	93	91	92	92	92	91	92	93
8	89	88	89	89	89	87	87	88
9	86	83	87	84	83	80	80	80
10	82	77	83	79	78	76	75	75
Ratio 10:1	1.60	1.75	1.58	1.70	1.78	1.87	1.98	2.01

that the polarisation of life chances was not just
affecting the most extreme group. At the other
extreme, the chances of premature death among
those living in areas with the best life chances
declined slightly, from 76% to 75% of the national
average. When comparing the very lowest
mortality decile to the highest mortality decile a
ratio can be used to illustrate the magnitude of the
difference between them. That ratio reached 2.01
by 1998 which means that people under the age
of 65 and living in the highest mortality areas of
Britain were, by then, *twice* as likely to die in
those years as were those under 65 and living in
the lowest mortality areas of Britain.
Geographical inequalities in health have never
been so wide.

This shocking statistic provides the premise for
the rest of the report.